M000221154

ANIMAL
TOTEMS

The Power and Prophecy of Your Animal Guides

Millie Gemondo and Trish MacGregor

FAIR WINDS
PRESS
GLOUCESTER, MASSACHUSETTS

Text © 2004 by Trish MacGregor and Millie Gemondo

First published in the USA in 2004 by
Fair Winds Press
33 Commercial Street
Gloucester, MA 01930

All rights reserved. No part of this book may be reproduced or utilized,
in any form or by any means, electronic or mechanical, without prior
permission in writing from the publisher.

08 07 06 05 04   1 2 3 4 5

ISBN 1-59233-044-4

Library of Congress Cataloging-in-Publication Data available

Cover illustration by Stefano Vitale
Cover design by John Hall Design Group
Book design by Laura Herrmann Design

Printed and bound in Canada

ANIMAL TOTEMS

To Al Zuckerman

With our deepest thanks and gratitude

CONTENTS

~~~~~~~~~~~~~~~~~~~~

~~~~~~~~~~~~~~~~~~~~

Authors'
Acknowledgments

~~~~~~~~~~~~~~~~~~~~~~~~~~~~~~

Millie wishes to thank Frank and Florence Gemondo, who taught her how to love animals and people. Frank passed away in 1961 and Florence passed away in 1996. She also wishes to thank her huge extended family, all of whom were cheering her on from the sidelines.

Trish wishes to thank Rob and Megan as well as her parents, Rose Marie and Tony Janeshutz, who always allowed her to indulge her love of animals.

We would both like to extend our deep thanks to our editor, Paula Munier.

Introduction

~~~~~~

We adopt them. We visit them in zoos. We *oohh* and *aahh* over them, cuddle them, live with them. In many instances they are our most intimate friends, our dearest companions. They fascinate us, heal us, teach us humility, compassion, unconditional love. Whether they are large or small or somewhere in between, fierce or domesticated, sly or comical, we are fascinated, sometimes scared, and always awed by animals.

Our connection with animals serves another, deeper function as well. Since ancient times, animals have been recognized as messengers, healers, and symbols of upcoming events and experiences. Paleolithic cave art suggests that early man considered animals as his link to Nature, to all of the mysterious forces that sculpted his life. Petroglyphs in Anasazi ruins in the American Southwest indicate a belief that animals were powerful, mysterious, connected to the divine. Among the ancient Egyptians, frogs were considered to be a symbol of fertility, cats were revered as guardian creatures and symbolized good fortune, and the falcon represented the flight of the soul after death. In ancient Greece, dolphins were believed to be Aphrodite's messengers and were associated with love, fertility, and passion. The Aztecs associated the butterfly with women who died at childbirth.

Many of these ancient beliefs about animals have survived to the present day, through folklore and ritual. During the Hopi's sacred dances, men impersonate kachina dolls—thought to be the spirit essence of everything in the real world—and three of these kachinas are butterflies, a prominent figure in Hopi myth. Among the Aymara of Bolivia, a rare nocturnal moth is thought to be an omen of death. In British mythology, the dog is believed to be capable of second sight. In the folklore of the North American Indians of the Central Plains, the coyote is considered to be a magician and trickster. In Hawaiian mythology, the shark is a symbol of power.

Today, we tend to dismiss the deeper meaning that animals bring into our lives. It isn't just that we're more distanced from Nature and natural forces than our ancestors were, but that we're so caught up in the business of living that we don't take the time to make the necessary connections. You walk into your living room one afternoon and find a snakeskin in the middle of the rug. A large snake skin. You freak. You grab the broom. You tear the living room apart, looking for the snake that shed its skin. And when you find the sucker, you either get it out of the house or kill it. When your spouse splits two days later with his mistress, you never draw the connection between this event and the snakeskin.

In the Bible, snakes symbolize temptation and forbidden knowledge. In ancient Greek and Roman cultures, snakes were symbols of the healing arts. The ancient symbol of the snake swallowing its own tail represents the way nature feeds on and renews itself. Psychologist Carl Jung considered snakes to be archetypal, representing an awareness of the essential energy of life and nature. The snake shedding its skin in your living room symbolized that some kind of transformative event was about to occur in your life and it would require that you "shed" an outdated belief or relationship.

In Jung's world, in the world of the ancients, the appearance of the snake wasn't random. It had *significance.* Jung called this phenomenon *synchronicity.* Physicist David Bohm, one of the pioneers in quantum physics, calls it the *implicate* or enfolded order, something that relates information about the deeper layers of our lives. Whatever we call it, synchronicity lies at the heart of our personal experiences with animals. Once we recognize the significance of the pattern the animal represents, we become participants in the deeper, underlying order of life.

How to Use This Book

When we brainstormed about how to arrange this book, we figured an alphabetical listing of animals would be the best way. But when friends and family began sharing their animal stories with us and asking about the deeper significance of their experiences, we realized the material would be more useful if it were arranged under broad archetypal meanings like *transformation, joy, romance, messengers.*

In Part Three, which covers more than a hundred animals, with short divinatory meanings for each one, the animals are arranged alphabetically. There's also an index.

We've attempted to provide broad archetypal meanings for each animal. But don't take these descriptions as the final meaning for your personal experiences. Use the descriptions as triggers for your own intuition. Jot notes in the section provided at the end of the book.

When we were deciding which animals to use, we tried to restrict the list to animals that most of us might encounter in our daily lives. However, more exotic animals enter our experiences through zoos, dreams, books, and movies, so we've also included some common exotics (now there's an oxymoron for you!) in Part Three.

Animal Rights

In any book about animals, the subject of animal rights usually surfaces. So, just for the record, we believe that every animal has the right to be treated humanely and compassionately.

Specifically, we don't condone hunting for sport nor do we condone blood sports like fox hunting, cock fighting, or bull fighting, or any other similar pursuit. We certainly don't condone hunting of any sort on private preserves, where aging zoo animals are shot for sport. While we understand the need for animal shelters, we don't condone euthanizing animals for convenience or just because they're taking up space in a shelter. Euthanasia should be used only if an animal is suffering. We don't condone the use of animals for the testing of drugs, cosmetics, or any other product, and we boycott products that use animals for testing.

When animals are raised for food, they should be treated humanely and compassionately. The treatment of chickens, for example, that John Robbins addresses in his landmark book, *Diet for a New America,* is not only cruel, but without conscience. The wholesale slaughter of cattle, lambs, turkeys, and other animals, without regard for their pain and suffering, has no place in a civilized society. Even a lobster shrieks when dropped alive into a pot of boiling water.

Yet, neither of us is a full-fledged vegetarian. We don't eat meat, but do eat fish and dairy products—though we are slowly weaning ourselves from those foods. We don't buy products that are derived from the suffering and inhumane treatment of animals. The bottom line for us is instinctive, intuitive. If it makes us cringe, we don't do it.

Both of us have animal companions. They are not pets or chattel. They are not our property. They are members of our families. They are friends, our mentors, our loved ones. They hog our beds at night. They peer over our shoulders or plop themselves in our laps as we read and write. They reflect who we are and who we are becoming—as people, as a species, as spiritual beings. They are the best of who we may one day be. It's miraculous that they put up with us and grace our lives with their presence.

We don't believe that violence of any kind serves a purpose. Animal rights activists who use violence to get their point across are just as guilty as warmongers who invade other countries for politics and profit. Pet owners who adopt a pet, then get bored with the animal or decide it doesn't fit into their lifestyle and return it to the shelter are just as just as guilty as the warmongers. It's the same mindset, just a different way of expressing it.

Change—*real* change, *lasting* change—begins in a family where the children have pets from whom they learn compassion, responsibility, and the deeper meaning of life. It begins in your ideals, in your diet, in your consumer choices. It begins with education. It begins with *you*.

PART ONE

DIVINATION & KINSHIP

"Freedom from exploitation and abuse by humankind should be the inalienable right of every living being. Animals are not there for us to drill holes into, clamp down, dissect, pull apart, render hopeless, and subject to agonizing experiments."

—From *When Elephants Weep: The Emotional Lives of Animals*, by Jeffrey Moussaieff Masson and Susan McCarthy

1

Patterns

I magine a summer day in your childhood. You and a friend are stretched out in the grass, watching the clouds that drift across the breathtakingly blue sky. A breeze nudges the clouds this way and that and pretty soon, they rearrange themselves into discernible shapes. An elephant, a dog, a tiger. And over there, to the east, a winged dinosaur takes flight toward the sun. Then the breeze eases the clouds apart and they re-form as something else.

For many of us, nature provided our earliest exposure to patterns—in the shapes of clouds in the sky or the shape of snowflakes on a window, in the tracks of a raccoon through the woods or the flight formation of geese winging their way elsewhere. Even if we were too young to understand the patterns, we recognized their beauty and their importance.

Since ancient times, man has looked to nature for hints about his own destiny, and many of those hints came through animals. Paleolithic cave art suggests that early man considered animals to be his link to nature, to all the mysterious forces that sculpted life. Petroglyphs in Anasazi ruins in the American Southwest indicated a belief that animals were man's connection to the divine. In ancient Greece, dolphins were believed to be Aphrodite's messengers and were associated with love, fertility, and passion. The appearance of a dolphin was cause for joy and celebration because it indicated a birth or a marriage. If ancient man could understand the meaning of what the appearance of a particular animal meant, he could understand the events and experiences that might be approaching for himself, his family, or his tribe.

In these indigenous traditions, the appearance of a particular animal in our lives, either in waking or dream states, carries a message, guidance, and answers specific to us and our personal situations. But we don't have to be shamans to learn how to interpret what that animal's appearance means. In fact, divination through our experiences with animals works exactly like any other kind of divination.

Synchronicity and Divination

You've been thinking about an old friend whom you haven't seen in twenty years. You simply can't get this person out of your mind. That evening, you receive an e-mail from your friend. Coincidence?

Swiss psychologist Carl Jung, in his 1949 foreword to the Richard Wilhelm edition of the *I Ching*, coined the word *synchronicity* to explain the workings of this ancient Chinese divination system. "…synchronicity takes the coincidence of events in space and time as meaning something more than mere chance, namely, a peculiar interdependence of objective events among themselves as well as with the subjective (psychic) states of the observer or observers."

Although Jung was addressing the specifics of the *I Ching*—the tossing of coins or yarrow sticks to create a particular pattern called a hexagram— synchronicity lies at the heart of every divination system. As soon as you toss coins, runes, dice, or lay down cards, they form a pattern intrinsic to that moment. The pattern is a reflection of some inner condition that is about to form or which already is forming in your life.

Divination through experiences with animals works in much the same way. In the moment of your experience, the *pattern* is apparent through the animal's habits and characteristics, the mythology and folklore about that animal, the circumstances surrounding your experience, the physical health of the animal, the myths and folklore associated with it, your feelings about the experience, the whole archetypal bundle.

The essential difference between animal divination and divination with inanimate objects lies in our emotional connections to animals. We cuddle a kitten or a puppy, but may be repulsed by the sight of a snake. Hummingbirds are pretty, vultures are sort of spooky, but neither presents the threat of a grizzly lumbering into our campsite in the dead of night. You get the idea. Our beliefs about animals influence our experiences with them.

Marie, a Belgian woman living in the U.S., detests snakes. After her divorce, a black snake took up residence in her yard. She didn't want to kill it. She's a vegetarian who abhors the killing of any animal, even those she detests. So for a long time, Marie and the snake coexisted. Then she realized that it was becoming bolder, moving closer to her house, her garage, watching her as she pruned bushes and trees. Then, one day, the snake tried to get into her car and not long afterward, she found its shedded skin on her living room floor.

At the time, she didn't think of the experience in terms of any message. She just wanted the snake out of her life and asked the manager of her building to kill it. In retrospect, however, she realized that if she had understood the experience as a divinatory tool, she might have gained insight and guidance about a situation that cropped up a short time later concerning a confrontation with authority.

In ancient Greek and Roman cultures, snakes were symbols of the healing arts. In Mayan art, the serpent is frequently portrayed and is perhaps most famous as Quezalcoatl, the feathered serpent. In the Bible, the snake symbolizes temptation and forbidden knowledge. Carl Jung considered snakes to be archetypal, a powerful symbol of the collective unconscious.

The essential message for Marie was enfolded in the characteristics of Snake, that it *must shed its skin for new growth to occur.* The snake was telling her that in order to heal and to move forward in her life, she had to shed old beliefs and habits. Even the animals we detest may act as messengers.

One evening while bike riding on dirt roads near their home, Rob and Trish came upon a small fox. It was just standing near a fence in the evening light, no more than five or six feet from where they were riding. In the year they had been biking the dirt roads, they had never seen a fox.

They paused to watch it for a few minutes, but as soon as they continued forward, the fox darted away and vanished into nearby woods.

They both sensed the sighting was significant, but weren't sure what it meant. Perhaps the answer lies in both the mythology and beliefs about foxes and in their inherent characteristics. In Japan, the fox is considered to be the most magical of creatures, a symbol of the harvest god, Inarti.

Among Native Americans, the fox was believed to protect families. The Hopi used fox furs for healing. The Incans revered the fox; it was one of the first creatures in their creation myths. Among some Native Americans, foxes are regarded as tricksters, shape-shifters, feminine magic.

Foxes are actually family creatures. They live in dens, where the male helps care for the young by providing food. Rather than forming packs, they keep to their single family units until it's time to oust their young.

At the time the couple sighted the fox, the main concern in their lives revolved around the woman's father, who had been living with the couple and their daughter for several years. They were preparing to move him to an assisted living facility where the woman's sister worked. He was eighty-eight years old, not well, widowed, and dreaded the move. But he needed more care than they could provide, so essentially the father was the "child being ousted from the nest."

The sighting turned out to be a perfect reflection of conditions in their lives at that time.

Frank Joseph, in his book, *Synchronicity & You,* calls such experiences Animal Ostenta, "a sign in the form of the coincidental, timely appearance of a creature that connects us with an event of personal significance." And in moments such as these, we are left with the sense that life is stranger and far more grand and mysterious than we thought possible.

Repeat Performances

One of the most intriguing facets of animal divination occurs when we have repeated experiences with the same type of animal over a period of several days or weeks.

Maureen, a homemaker in the Midwest, spent a small fortune on impatiens one spring, which she planted in her backyard. As soon as she had planted them, a mole took up residence in the impatiens. He had a grand old time, burrowing through the freshly planted impatiens until the flowers were ruined and the yard had so many molehills in it that it looked like the surface of the moon. Maureen leveled the yard, replanted her impatiens, but the mole tore up this batch as well. The message?

Let's take a deeper look at Mole. What do his habits and characteristics tell us? He doesn't just burrow. He's acutely adapted to life underground, in the dark. He's blind, yet has many sensory organs that enable him to survive underground. He creates a labyrinth of tunnels in his dark, underground world, using his front legs to dig and his hind legs to shovel dirt behind him as he tunnels. In terms of folklore and mythology, the Lakota Indians believed that Mole was caretaker of the earth and could sense any disturbance that was stirring in the depths of the planet, such as earthquakes and volcanic eruptions. To them, Mole was in touch with the earth's pain, illness, and discomforts.

Based just on this, Mole's repeated appearance indicated that she needed to pay closer attention to her physical health. She had high blood pressure and blood sugar at the time and knew that she should get more exercise. She was also becoming well-known in her area as an intuitive counselor, so Mole's appearance seemed to be confirming this direction in her life and under-scoring the importance of her intuition.

Repetition of an experience with an animal often occurs when a single experience involves two or more of the same animal. A family returned from a vacation to find a dead tree frog in their family room and several ceramic frogs that were part of a collection shattered in the same area as the dead frog. The husband, wife, and child all felt uneasy about the dead and broken frogs, but weren't sure why. Within twenty-four hours, the family received news that the husband's father had had a massive stroke and was dying.

In this incident, the location of the dead frog and the shattered ceramic frogs seemed to be as telling as the repetition of the frog pattern: the family room. A member of the family had died.

This doesn't mean that every dead animal we see spells the death of someone we love. It may mean the end of a job or a relationship or a move away from a place we have loved. Or perhaps we've reached a crossroad of some sort in life, and when we make a choice, the path not taken closes off. Everything about the experience has to be considered: the state of the animal, how we feel about what has happened and about the animal, the physical location where the experience occurred, who else was involved, perhaps even the time of the day and the weather.

Pets

"I want a dog. Can I have a kitten?"

"Oh, that bird is so cute. Can we get it?"

Anyone with kids can attest to the persistence of children when it comes to having a pet. If you give in, then the main issue becomes which pet? Which animal?

The selection itself often holds a greater significance than simply acquiring a pet. For a family that welcomes a dog into its midst, the deeper meaning may concern issues of loyalty and unconditional love. Dogs have been around since at least 7500 B.C., when they were domesticated in ancient Egypt. In Egyptian myth, the dog was sacred to the god Anubis. The dog was revered in Babylonia, was an emblem of the Phoenician physician Gala, and is associated with Artemis in Greek mythology. Australian Aborigines consider the dog an essential companion, In folklore, dogs are believed to have second sight and are able to see ghosts, spirits, and deities.

For a family that selects a guinea pig, the characteristics of the animal as well as native lore may hold vital clues about its significance. In some parts of South America, it's believed that guinea pigs can heal illness and appease negative spirits. In the wild, they are social animals that live in groups called herds. Since they don't have natural defenses, they use the herd as protection. The significance, then, may be that the family needs to bind together and be more protective of each other or they need to open up their lives to other people whose beliefs and goals are similar.

We recently met a family that had acquired a rabbit. The son was crazy about this rabbit. He attended to it with care and great diligence, played with it, even took it with him on vacation. A kid and his rabbit, you might say, big deal. Was there a deeper significance?

Besides being cute and furry, rabbits are known for being prolific. Their young are capable of being on their own within twenty-eight days, a lunar cycle. They move quickly and abruptly unless they're scared, and then they freeze. Unknown to the boy, his parents had been trying to have a second child for several years and were now considering other alternatives—fertility treatments, in vitro, adoption. But they felt uneasy about the alternatives. They needed more time to consider their options.

About a month after the boy acquired the rabbit, the woman discovered that she was pregnant. Today, the boy has a sister.

The significance of the rabbit for this family happened to be very straightforward. Just because your family acquires a rabbit, however, doesn't necessarily mean that someone is going to get pregnant. But it usually indicates that you should take a wait and see attitude about something that makes you feel uneasy. It indicates fertility, new vistas and possibilities, and is also an indicator of time, specifically the lunar month.

Whether you're thinking of getting a pet or already own pets, take a deeper look at what the animal might mean in terms of where you are in your life at this moment—and where you would like to be. Chances are, the animal is a faithful reflection of some inner condition in your life.

Flipper and Friends

In the early sixties, scientist John Lily set up a habitat in the U.S. Virgin Islands that enabled him to live closely with dolphins. His discoveries about their intelligence, their complex social interactions, how they rear their young, and the apparent spiritual component in their lives, subsequently led to research facilities where ordinary people could swim with dolphins. The anecdotal evidence about these human/dolphin interactions is rich and varied.

"I swim with dolphins several times a year," says Vivian, a psychiatric nurse. "It's part of my spiritual practice. The experience is always uplifting and enormously healing."

"It was the most extraordinary thing I ever experienced," says Luis, a computer programmer.

"It was awesome," says thirteen-year-old Hans.

Awesome, extraordinary, healing, incredible, indescribable, fantastic. That's what we heard when we talked to people who had gone swimming with dolphins. Some people swim with dolphins for the same reason that other people skydive or climb Mount Everest, because the opportunity is there, because it's thrilling. They do it for the experience. But then there are people like Vivian, who swim with dolphins because it brings something positive into their lives, a spiritual and healing dimension that is difficult to describe because it's so ephemeral. And for these people, the significance of the experience is perhaps best defined by the mammal's characteristics.

Thanks to John Lily and the researchers that have followed him, we know that dolphins are *communicators*. Those clicks and whistles and physical antics are their language. Anecdotal evidence of their compassion and altruism has even reached the evening news. When young Elian Gonzalez fled Cuba on a rickety boat with his mother, the boat sank and everyone perished except for Elian, who was rescued and kept alive by a pod of dolphins. The fact that he was aided by dolphins added to the overall mystique that he was destined for something special.

We know that dolphins are sexual, sensual, and playful and that their young are birthed underwater, with the help of nursemaids who remain close to the mother. We know they're intelligent, that autistic and handicapped children respond to them, and that dolphins, through their sonar, are able to sense physical ailments in people.

In mythology and folklore, the dolphin has a long and distinguished history. In Greek myth, dolphins were associated with Apollo. Poseidon is said to have placed the dolphin in the heavens as a constellation (Delphinus) because a dolphin saved the bard Arion from death by pirates. Celtic lore connects the dolphin with the power of the water. Among some Aboriginal tribes, the dolphin is a totem. Among some South American tribes, the river dolphin is believed to be a shape-shifter that takes human form when the moon is full.

So when we consciously interact with dolphins, we actually may be seeking an expansion of spiritual awareness, playfulness, sexuality. We may be looking for new ways to communicate who we are and how we interact with groups. We may be consciously seeking to heal a wound.

Any time we consciously seek interaction with an animal, whether it's a dolphin or a dog, it's to our advantage to look for the deeper meaning.

Intuition

Your intuition plays a vital role in understanding the deeper significance of your experiences with animals. The in-depth divinatory meanings provided in Part Two and the briefer meanings in Part Three are the most common ones that we've discovered. By no means should you limit yourself to them. Use them as guidelines, as triggers, and let your own intuition guide you. As your experiences with animals deepen and expand, so will your divinatory meanings.

The most important attributes you can bring to animal divination are an open mind, a willingness to experiment, keen observation, a sense of playfulness, and trust in your intuitive abilities. To get started, try the brainstorming activity on the following page. It will acquaint you with your deeper feelings about animals in general and will stimulate memories of experiences you may have had with animals that held a deeper significance, even if you didn't realize it at the time.

Brainstorming Activity 1

This activity is designed to stimulate your intuition. As you go through the list of questions, jot down whatever comes to mind. By answering without giving it too much thought, you're allowing your intuitive self to speak.

1. If I could be an animal, it would be _____ . Why?

2. Describe a memorable experience you've had with an animal. It can be any animal, any memory, good or bad.

   _____

   _____

   _____

   _____

   _____

3. What was going on in your life at the time you had this experience?

   _____

   _____

4. List five animals and what they represent to you.

   _____

   _____

   _____

   _____

   _____

5. What animals do you consider to be powerful? Why?

   _____

   _____

   _____

6. Which animals fascinate you?

_____

_____

_____

7. Which animals repel you? Why?

_____

_____

_____

8. Toward which animals do you feel utter indifference? Why?

_____

_____

_____

9. In general, what role do animals play in your life?

_____

_____

_____

10. Do you feel you communicate with your animal companions? Or that they communicate with you? If so, how?

_____

_____

11. Give one example of a time when you sought out an experience of some kind with an animal. This can be anything from a swim with dolphins to a trip to the pound.

_____

_____

_____

Ants to Zebras

When we were selecting animals for our in-depth divinatory descriptions, we tried to choose animals that are common to daily life. Even though some people work with exotic animals or may visit a zoo on a daily basis, most of us don't. So it's unlikely that we would have an experience with a zebra or an elephant, a lion or a giraffe. Exotic animals are included primarily in Chapter Fourteen, "Endangered Animals."

The types of birds on the planet are so numerous that an entire book could be devoted just to their divinatory meaning. So we've included common wild birds as well as birds that people are most likely to have as pets. If you happen to run into a dodo bird, you're on your own as to what it might mean!

2

Animal Talk

~~~~~~~~~~~~~~~~~~~~~~~~~~~~~~~~~~

Your dog whines and looks at you with those big liquid eyes.

Your cat snakes between your legs, purring or meowing *for something*. The panther at the zoo paces restlessly from one end of its cage to the other.

The alligator in the lake near your home swims languidly through warm sunlight, its eyes always just above the surface of the water, watching you watching him.

The spider on your porch spins its exquisite web but freezes as soon as you get too close to the web.

In each instance, the animal is speaking. *I'm hungry. I want to be hugged. Let me outta here. I am patient. Are you edible?* The meanings we assign to animal behavior, sounds, and movements are based on our experiences and may not have anything to do with what the animal is trying to communicate. Then again, perhaps the animal's behavior is intended precisely for us.

Yeah, right, you reply.

You may be able to identify with something that your dog or your cat is feeling, but what do you have in common with an alligator or a spider?

~~~~~~~~~~~~~~~~~~~~~~~~~~~~~~~~~~

You're both predators, that's what. You are cunning and deceptive, infinitely patient when you want something, and you act on instinct. You're about survival of the fittest, Darwin's theories in action.

Animal talk may be the sound of birds at sunrise or the purr of a cat as it snuggles up next to you. But it also may be that alligator, lying in wait, or that spider, weaving miracles on your porch, or a fox, frozen in the twilight in your backyard. The talk of animals bears no relation to language as we speak or understand it. *We have a thought, our vocal cords move, we speak.*

If we are to understand what animals have to teach us, then we must observe, scrutinize, decipher. We must learn silence and stillness. We must become the Sherlock Holmes who collects clues, leads, bits of information about the animals that grace our lives. To some extent, we must learn who they are from their perspective, and this requires trust.

"If an animal can trust us, we can trust the universe," writes Margot Lasher in her wonderful book, *And the Animals Will Teach You.*

Understanding the animal talk of our pets is one thing, but understanding it in other animals is something else. When you attract repeated experiences with a particular animal, then this animal is speaking to you in a symbolic way. To decipher the symbolism—and get the message—it's necessary to have some idea what you feel about the particular animal. In the brainstorming activity on the following page, jot a word or phrase that pinpoints your feeling about the animal. Don't think too much about it; write the first thing that comes to mind. If snakes instill fear in your heart and make you want to run, then put that down. What we're after here is your visceral response to various animals.

Brainstorming Activity 2

Animal	*Your feelings about it*
1. ant	
2. bear	
3. cat	
4. chicken	
5. cow	
6. crow	
7. deer	
8. dog	
9. dolphin	
10. duck	
11. eagle	
12. elephant	
13. flea	
14. fox	
15. frog	
16. gull	
17. iguana	
18. insects	
19. lion	
20. lizard	
21. monkey	

Animal	Your feelings about it
22. mouse	
23. opossum	
24. otter	
25. pig	
26. quail	
27. rabbit	
28. raccoon	
29. rat	
30. raven	
31. robin	
32. rodents	
33. shark	
34. sheep	
35. snake	
36. skunk	
37. swallow	
38. swan	
39. tiger	
40. turtle	
41. wasp	
42. wolf	
43. zebra	

The Power of Attraction

The abbreviated list above will give you some idea of how deeply embedded your ideas and beliefs are about animals, even those you may not think about consciously. These ideas and beliefs, in turn, act like a magnet for attracting certain animals. Sometimes, the information we need comes to us through an animal that is sure to seize our attention. A cat or a dog walking into your den won't be as startling as a mouse that one of your cats brings home and which then scurries into your den to hide behind your desk.

Not too long ago, one of Trish's cats came racing into the house with a mouse, very proud of herself for having done her cat thing. The mouse was still alive, got loose, and raced into Trish's den to hide out. It took several hours to move furniture around and chase the mouse out of its hiding place and outdoors. The message?

Mice are all about details—tending to them or being lost so deeply inside them that you can't see the larger picture. Since this happened in Trish's den, where she works, she felt sure the message was related to details concerning work. At the time, she was in the midst of a novel where certain details weren't panning out the way she'd planned because she didn't have the bigger picture. While she would have figured this out sooner or later on her own, the incident with the mouse brought the point home in a way that she couldn't ignore.

Another example happened while we were working on the dragonfly section of Chapter Five ("Messengers"). One day, Trish's husband, Rob, walked outside and immediately saw four dragonflies hovering and darting around the pool in the backyard. Although dragonflies are fairly common in Florida, it's somewhat unusual to find them around a swimming pool at twilight. We all figured the dragonfly sighting meant Rob would be receiving news or a message soon, the general meaning of a dragonfly. But what possible message could be associated with a swimming pool, traditionally associated with pleasure, warm weather, and health/exercise?

As it turned out, the news concerned finances—a check arrived in the mail and a woman whom he was certifying in yoga (health) paid him what she owed him. Could he have figured this out based just on the clues? Probably not. There are times when your encounter or experience with an animal alerts you that something is coming up, but exactly what that something might be remains a complete mystery. You simply have to wait and see.

Guidelines for Interpreting Your Encounter

When you have an encounter or experience with an animal, your interpretation of the event should be a process. Rather than leaping to conclusions about what it might mean, take note of the following details:

- *Your initial reaction.* Were you delighted? Terrified? Mystified? Disgusted? Your reaction tells you a great deal about your ideas and core beliefs concerning the animal. Remember: You attract the particular animal through your deepest beliefs about the animal, but also about your view of the world and yourself.

- *Where the encounter occurs.* If the encounter occurs in the animal's natural habitat, then it's probably less meaningful than one elsewhere. If the animal is way out of its element, the experience may be exceptionally meaningful for you.

- *When the experience occurred.* The time of day or night, the season, even the weather can hold vital clues about the significance of the encounter.

- *How you feel.* This one is important. How you feel about an experience with an animal is especially revealing. Were you afraid? Apprehensive? Joyful? Sad? Quite often, your emotions are your most direct link to the meaning of the encounter.

- *Who you're with.* Sometimes, this can be as significant as the encounter itself. If you're with other people when the encounter happens, your relationship with them can lead you into the heart of the meaning.

- *What you're doing at the time of the encounter.* Your activity at the time of the encounter is another signpost. Are you driving? Walking? Hiking? Making love? Arguing? Crying? If you're dreaming, then note every detail you can recall about the dream and attempt to interpret it according to symbols that are unique to your dreams.

- *Keep a journal of your encounters.* Once you begin paying attention to what physicist David Bohm calls the implicate or hidden order of life, then you're inviting more experiences of this kind. It's as if you're wearing a huge sign around your neck that shouts to the universe, Hey, I'm ready, bring on the mystery, the wonder, the joy.

PART TWO

THE ANIMALS

"In the United States alone, it is estimated that more than seventy million animals are used annually in research, and that one animal dies every three seconds, often in pain and fear."

—From *The Ten Trusts,*
by Jane Goodall and Marc Bekoff

The material in this section is arranged under broad headings that depict the divinatory meanings of the various animals. Under "Transformation," the title of Chapter Three, for example, you'll find butterfly, frog, and snake. These are not the only animals that embody the idea of transformation, but they are the most common.

In the interest of space, we have provided at least one in-depth look at an animal in each chapter. These sections include the mythology and folklore associated with an animal as well as facts and trivia about the animal. All the animals in Part Two, however, are explored in depth in terms of their divinatory meanings.

As you're reading through these descriptions and meanings in each chapter, the names of other animals will come to mind. Jot them in the spaces provided at the end of the chapters. Use these animals as a springboard for your own exploration.

3

Transformation

BUTTERFLY, FROG, SNAKE

To transform means to change from the inside out, to be made over so completely that you're old self is unrecognizable. Plastic surgery might do it, except that beneath the new face, you're pretty much the same person. The kind of transformation so prevalent in mythology, folklore, and fairy tales is profound and irreversible.

An insect lays eggs. The eggs hatch as larva or caterpillars. The caterpillars eat constantly, preparing themselves for the pupa stage, when they won't be able to eat at all. Since they consume so much, they grow rapidly and shed their chitkin skin four or five times before their pupa skin develops and then hardens. The pupal stage can last anywhere from a week to several months or up to seven years if the pupa hibernates. When an insect emerges from the chrysalis, the change is profound and irreversible. Who would recognize him? He or she has gone from a creepy crawler, earthbound and ugly, to a magnificent creature that takes to the skies.

The frog lays eggs. The eggs hatch as tadpoles, water-breathing creatures with gills and long tails and fins. The metamorphosis from tadpole to frog happens rapidly, in a matter of days. They lose their gills, their tails are absorbed, they grow webbed feet. Again, the change is profound and irreversible.

The transformation in snakes is also dramatic. From the moment a snake is born to the moment it dies, it never stops growing. So when it sheds, it literally has outgrown its own skin. In some species, the shedding of skin occurs every twenty days and it usually comes off in one piece, including the hard, transparent spectacles, which protect the snake's eyes. Profound, irreversible change.

Insect, amphibian, reptile. The butterfly, the frog, and the snake are as different from each other as the moon is from the sun. Yet, each embodies the theme of transformation.

BUTTERFLY

Myths, Folklore, Legends

Native American myths are filled with butterfly lore. In a legend of the Papago, the creator felt sorry for children because he realized they would grow old and wrinkled and eventually die. To make them happy, he collected magnificent colors from sunlight, trees and flowers, the sky and seas, and put them into a magical bag that he presented to the children. When they opened the bag, colored butterflies fluttered out, the most beautiful things the children had ever seen. In this legend, the butterflies were also able to sing, which made the birds jealous. So the creator took away their ability to sing.

The obsidian butterfly is a patron deity, Itzpapalotl, in the Aztec calendar. The Aztecs also believed that butterflies were actually the spirits of their loved ones, visiting to assure them they were happy and well in the afterlife. Among one Colombian tribe, a large white moth found in a bedroom is actually the spirit of an ancestor dropping in for a visit. Among the Hopi, the transformative power of the butterfly is embodied in one of their sacred dances, the Butterfly Dance. It's also personified in kachina dolls, figures carved by the Hopi which represent the spiritual essence of everything in the physical universe.

For Native Americans, the butterfly is primarily a symbol of resurrection. Among certain indigenous tribes in Colombia, butterflies are associated with fertility, because they pollinate plants, and with shamans, because of their ability to metamorphose.

Facts & Trivia

There are more than 24,000 species of butterflies in the world and 140,000 species of moths. They populate every continent except Antarctica.

All butterflies and moths go through three distinct stages—caterpillar, chrysalis, and the final birth into splendor. They are migratory insects, with the Monarch as the undisputed winner, regularly migrating between southern Canada and central Mexico, a distance of more than 2,500 miles. This migration seems to be genetically implanted. A mother Monarch may lay her eggs in route, die, and then her hatchlings continue the journey. Monarchs weigh about a fifth of an ounce, yet they can fly at speeds of up to twenty miles an hour and at heights of 10,000 feet. The fastest Lepidoptera (the order of insects including butterflies and moths) is the sphinx moth, clocked at thirty-seven miles an hour and able to hover like a helicopter.

Since 1983, the Monarchs have been an endangered species. Recently in Mexico, thousands of Monarchs were found dead from an unknown cause. Entomologists suspect that climate change may be at fault, pointing out another fact about butterflies: They are indicators of the health or illness of the environment.

The motif of butterflies as symbolic of profound transformation has certainly made its way into the modern world. On the Internet, we found a site for survivors of cardiac failure called The Butterfly Project. "When we face heart failure, we may start to question our assumptions about the world and ourselves, and we may discover that our priorities shift as we begin to realize what is most important to us," writes Dr. Steve Serr, the contact person for the site. "If you are a cardiac survivor, or have been caring for a survivor who has been trying to find a way to understand, digest, and grow from such life-changing experiences, then this project is for you."

We also found a site called The Butterfly Celebration, a company that specializes in releasing live butterflies at special events like weddings, anniversaries, weddings, and other occasions that represent transformative landmarks in our lives.

Significance

Key Words: Transformation, metamorphosis, fertility, soaring

The Big Picture: It's time to release your old self and move into a new chapter of your life. To begin this new journey, it's important to be open to every offer and opportunity. Butterflies sometimes symbolize messages. If a Monarch butterfly flies through your window today, then start packing for a long trip!

Romance: The love of your life may be just around the next corner. You're attractive to the opposite sex right now, so take advantage of it. A butterfly's meaning in this area signals a profound change in your marital status. If you're happily married, however, then perhaps your relationship is entering a newer, even better phase.

Finances: A time of change. Embrace new opportunities. Your ideas are flowing now and they are innovative and cutting edge. Let your intuition and instincts guide you.

Work/Career: A profound change is in the wind. If you dislike your day job, then resign before you get fired. If you love what you do, then be assured that at this time you can reach for your dreams and achieve them. You can soar.

Health: You may be coming out of a challenging phase with your health. Like the cardiac survivors in The Butterfly Project, your experiences have caused you to realize what is really important in your life. Now step forward with strength and optimism to begin the next phase of your life.

Family: Perhaps you moved recently. Or your household changed in some way—a new child, an elderly parent moving in, a cousin who is staying with you. Whatever the change, it's important that you embrace it rather than resist.

Creativity: Your creativity is entering a new phase. If you have finished a novel or screenplay, a butterfly's appearance bodes well for a sale. If you've been thinking about writing a novel or screenplay, then get started. There's no time like the present, isn't that how the saying goes? No matter what you do in this area, now is the time to reach for your dreams and make them happen.

Spirituality: You're on a new path now. Your inner guidance and intuition are exceptionally strong. Take up meditation or yoga. Go within.

FROG

Myths, Folklore, Legends

The tale of The Frog Prince is probably one of the most famous fairy tales in the Western world. It's also a simple tale. A princess is wooed by a frog, who asks for a kiss. The princess recoils in horror, then gradually consents to kiss the frog, probably out of pity. The moment she kisses him, he's transformed into a handsome prince and the two are married. The moral is that beauty is hidden beneath an ugliness that is only skin deep. Or, don't judge a frog—or anyone else—based on looks.

In the version of the fairy tale by the Brothers Grimm, the princess isn't quite as passive. A young princess was so beautiful (of course) that the sun itself was astonished whenever it shone on her face. Near her father's castle lay a great dark forest (of course) and when the days were warm, the princess used to go there and sit by a cool fountain. When she was bored, she brought her golden ball with her and tossed it up high in the air.

One day, she failed to catch the ball and it rolled away and into the water. It sank and she began to cry, and then a voice asked her why she was crying. She glanced in the direction of the voice and saw a big, ugly frog sticking its head up out of the water. She told the frog what had happened and he said he would retrieve her ball, but wanted to know what she would give him in return. She promised she would give the frog whatever he wanted. And what he wanted was to be her companion.

She promised that, but thought how silly it was, a frog asking to be the companion of a human being. The frog kept his end of the bargain and when he asked the girl to help him out of the water and take him up to the castle, she ran away. The next day, however, the dripping wet frog appeared at the castle door. The girl told her father, the king, what had happened and he told her that since she had made a promise, she had to keep it. Much to her disgust, she had to bring the frog inside the castle and, later, into her room.

The frog insisted on being brought into her bed and threatened to tell her father if she didn't comply. She was so angry she grabbed the frog and hurled him against the wall. But when he hit the floor, he was no longer a frog but a prince. And by her father's will, he became not only her companion, but her husband.

In ancient Egypt, the frog was a symbol of fertility, water, and renewal. Each year when the Nile flooded, frogs appeared in massive numbers and became associated with abundance and rain because the flooding of the Nile was so crucial to agriculture.

In pre-Columbian Mesoamerica, many tribes worshipped a goddess known as Ceneotl, the patron of childbirth and fertility, who took the form of a frog or toad with many udders. The symbol of fertility is also found in Greek and Roman myths, where the frog is associated with Aphrodite/Venus.

For the early Aztecs, the toad was Tialtecuhti, the earth mother goddess, who personified the cycle of death and rebirth. It was widely believed among the Aztecs that toads were the guardians of the underworld.

Among Native Americans, the frog is the preeminent symbol celebrating the fertility of the wetlands. It's also considered to be symbolic of the shaman's power of transformation.

In ancient Chinese tales and legends, the toad is a trickster and magician, but he's also the keeper of the most powerful secrets of the world, like the secret of immortality.

Another facet of frogs in myths and legends involves their alchemical ability. They are purveyors of poison or powerful drugs, which can heal or induce hallucinations. Some native tribes in South America use toad and frog poisons in their spiritual rituals, to induce vision quests. Ironically, the chemical secreted by the Poison Dart Frog may be useful as a cardiac stimulant for heart attack patients and another produces a painkiller that may someday replace morphine.

Facts & Trivia

Frogs are ancient. For 190 million years, the ancestors of the modern frog roamed the planet, looking pretty much as they do now. The Ichthyostega, the prehistoric predecessor of the modern frog, lived 370 million years ago, during the Devonian Period, and their skeletal remains were first found in Greenland. The secret to their success is their adaptability. The fact that they are amphibious is a tremendous advantage; they can live in both worlds.

Frogs are found anywhere that has fresh water, on every continent except Antarctica. They thrive in damp, tropical climates, but also live in deserts and on 15,000-foot mountain slopes. The Australian water-holding frog lives in the desert and survives by burrowing underground and surrounding itself with its own shedded skin. It can wait up to seven years for rain. Frogs eat almost anything, from insects to snails to small fish. Some of the larger varieties, like the horned frog of Argentina, consume a mouse in a single mouthful.

Generally, frogs don't have teeth. Some don't even have sticky tongues; they catch their prey with their feet. Frog's huge eyes are a distinct advantage. These allow him to see a vast spectrum of color and to see well in dim light. The eyes also help in swallowing by sinking through openings in the skull, which helps force the food down their throats.

The frog drinks and breathes through his skin. Although he has lungs, he relies on the extra oxygen absorbed through his skin, especially when he's underwater. About once a week, a frog sheds his skin, just like a snake. He twists, he stretches, loosening the old skin, and then he pulls it off over his head and eats it. All frogs have poison glands in their skin, but most of the time, the poison isn't strong enough to discourage predators. The Poison Dart Frog, which comes in 170 different varieties, is an exception. Its name comes from the fact that native people use its poison on the tips of arrows and darts. The most dangerous one is the golden poison frog, which contains enough poison to kill eight people.

If you walk down to a pond on a still night, the air is exploding with a cacophony of sounds: the mating call of male frogs. The ears of frogs, called tympanum, resemble two flat circles, and are located behind the eyes. The size of the tympanum and the distance between them determines which sounds a frog will hear best and helps the females identify and locate the males of her species. As the female lays her eggs, the male frog, perched on her back, releases sperm that fertilizes them. There can be anywhere from one to hundreds or thousands, but few survive the journey to life.

Three to twenty-five days after the eggs are laid, they hatch. As tadpoles. Like caterpillars, tadpoles are voracious eaters, storing up on anything and everything that will fuel their metamorphosis. Within several weeks, the hind legs sprout. Then the lungs develop and the front legs appear. The tail gradually shrinks until it's completely absorbed into the body. Most frogs are lousy parents. They abandon the eggs as soon as they are laid. But a few breeds have developed meticulous ways to care for their young. The marsupial frog keeps her eggs in a pouch, much like a kangaroo, until they hatch into tadpoles. The Surinam toad carries her young embedded in the skin of her back. The gastric brooding frog of Australia swallows her fertilized eggs and the tadpoles stay in her stomach for up to eight weeks. They finally hop out of her mouth as tiny frogs.

Frogs are an "indicator species," meaning that they are the first to be affected by changes in the environment. Their rapidly dwindling numbers is a warning that our planet may be evolving into an inhospitable place.

Significance

Key Words: Transformation, metamorphosis, adaptability, camouflage, fertility, good luck, fortune, healing, rain, emotions

The Big Picture: You are entering a new period in your personal or professional life. This is a fertile time for new projects and new ideas. The frog helps you to cope with change and to make the transition smoothly. This is a period of healing, cleansing, and spiritual awakening. Luck is on your side.

Take note of the context in which your frog experience occurs. Are you outside or inside? Is the frog in a particular room or area of your home or office? What's the frog doing? How do you feel about the experience? Are you and the frog near a body of water? These kinds of details provide deeper significance to the experience.

If you dream of a frog, that's about as good as it gets. However, notice what's going on in the dream, what the frog is doing, how the frog looks, and how you feel about the dream when you wake. Apply the same attention to the frog in a dream as you would in waking life.

Romance: Don't judge a frog by its looks! The love of your life may be right in front of you. He or she may be someone you already know. Even if you don't see anyone who interests you at the moment, trust that the person is about to enter your life. If you're already committed or married, your relationship enters new territory, a new creative cycle.

Finances: The check isn't just in the mail. It's probably already in your mailbox. Your finances improve through unexpected sources of income that show up very soon. Be on the lookout for new financial and investment opportunities. A raise may in the offing.

Work/Career: If you like your job, things are likely to improve where you work. You may get a promotion or a bonus. If, however, you're bored or dislike your work, then new professional opportunities will present themselves. The frog's physical condition and the circumstances of your experience with the frog will reveal the nature of what's coming up.

Health: The significance in terms of health depends on the frog's location. If the frog is in your family room and looks to be in good physical condition, then the family's overall health is good and will get better. The reverse is also true. If the frog is dead, then this may signal the death of someone close to you. Use your intuition to divine the deeper meaning.

Family: If there's someone of childbearing age in the house, the frog's appearance often means pregnancy or an uncomplicated childbirth. Family relationships improve and enter a period of rebirth and renewed understanding.

Creativity: You're on a roll. Go with the flow and trust your innate creative ability. Due to the frog's sensitive tympanic organ, it's important at this time to listen for the song that is uniquely yours and to express it honestly. Communication is heightened.

Spirituality: You enter a period of spiritual renewal and rebirth. Your intuition is expanding and deepening. You become more aware of your dreams and their meaning. You may decide to take workshops or attend seminars in dream recall and interpretation.

SNAKE

Myths, Folklore, Legends

Snake appears in the myths and legends of nearly every culture. To Christians, it is an evil tempter in league with Satan, a symbol of forbidden knowledge. To the ancient Greeks, it represented healing and occult knowledge.

The Incas believed the snake stood for knowledge. In ancient Egypt, the Cobra symbolized immortality and was a protected deity. One of the most famous snakes in legends is the plumed serpent, Quetzacoatl, a deity of the Aztecs.

In Chinese mythology, the world is surrounded by a pair of intertwined snakes, which symbolize the power and wisdom of the creator.

Buddha was supposedly attacked by a snake that wound itself seven times around his waist. Because of Buddha's inner strength, the snake couldn't kill him and became his follower. In this way, Snake helped Buddha attain a higher level of self-realization. In Kundalini yoga, practitioners strive to awaken energy that is coiled within them like a snake. As the energy is awakened, it is brought up through the chakras to the third eye.

In Hindu mythology, the serpent represents creative power and is a manifestation of the Vedic Agni as fire. The cobra is the mount of Vishnu, and he sleeps on the coiled serpent of the waters.

The serpent as divinity is found in ancient Persia, through the great sky serpent Azhi Dahaka, the creator of all the planets in the sky. In early Mideastern myths, the serpent is also lord of the waters. The serpent as the thirst-quenching rainbow occurs in Indian, Amerindian, Australian, and African legend; it is also a sky-hero and creator. In African tribes the snake can be a royal emblem, an incarnation of the dead, or a mythical ancestor.

Celtic tradition connects the serpent with the healing waters and with the Great Mother Bridget. In this mythology, snakes spell trouble. Wherever they appear, strife and infertility are just around the corner. Even King Arthur had trouble with snakes. About the time that Mordred was conceived, Arthur dreamed of dragons and serpents. This motif was repeated during Arthur's last dream, when he was devoured by the serpents and dragons— and subsequently killed by Mordred in his final battle.

Facts & Trivia

There are 2,500 different species of snakes. All of them are carnivorous and eat a vast spectrum of animal life, from insects to frogs, rats and even other snakes. About twenty percent of them are poisonous, with the black and green mamba as among the most poisonous. Both produce neurotoxins that paralyze and kill the prey swiftly.

Poisonous snakes have two hollow, hypodermic-like teeth—fangs—in the front of the upper jaw. In some snakes, like vipers, the fang-bearing bone is attached to the skull in such a way that the fangs can be moved back up against the roof of the mouth when not in use. Cobras and coral snakes represent another large group of snakes in which the fangs are constantly erect. The fangs connect by the venom duct to the two venom glands, which are modified salivary glands on each side of the head behind the eyes.

Short-range vision is well developed in most snakes, but those that burrow may be completely blind. They have a powerful sense of smell. A snake's constantly flicking tongue carries scent particles to a specialized sensory organ on the roof of the mouth. Snakes are deaf to airborne sounds, but thanks to their well-developed nervous systems they feel vibrations in the ground. Pit vipers and some boas and pythons have a heat receptor that detects small differences in temperature. This enables them to locate and capture warm-blooded prey at night.

The snake's anatomy enables free movement. The skeleton is light, with anywhere from 100 to 300 vertebrae. Each vertebra is connected to a pair of ribs on either side of the body. The first two vertebrae are connected to the head rather than to the ribs. The snake's skull is loosely built, making it easier to swallow large prey.

In fiction, the healing symbolism of snakes is beautifully portrayed in Vonda McIntyre's Nebula award–winning novel, *Snake*.

Significance

Key Words: Power, transformation, shedding, rebirth, healing, spirituality, intuition

The Big Picture: Expect profound change in some area of your life. Snake is always yang (male energy) and may relate to a husband, father, or brother. Or it may be addressing the yang energy in yourself or in someone close to you. The type of snake and where you see it are important. If the snake is in your house, connect the meaning to what it's doing and what the room represents to you.

A rattler indicates a spiritual quest of some kind and an emphasis on nocturnal activities—lucid dreaming, vivid dream recall, astral travel. A garter snake suggests help from someone close to you. A common black snake symbolizes sexuality—yours or someone else's—or that sexual issues are involved. Any kind of snake indicates healing and power.

Romance: Your sex life heats up. Passion soars to the forefront of your life. If you find a snake's skin, then perhaps you need to re-evaluate an existing relationship. Have you outgrown the relationship?

Finances: A profound change in your income or in your spouse's income is indicated. This can be either positive or challenging, depending on the type of snake and the location of the experience.

Work/Career: If you've been thinking about changing work or careers, the appearance of Snake suggests that the change is just around the corner. Take advantage of an opportunity. Don't procrastinate.

Health: If you've been ill or are recovering from an illness or injury, then expect vast improvement and healing on many levels. Snake's appearance can also indicate that someone around you is being healed. Again, the details surrounding your experience hold vital clues to its meaning.

Family: Awakening sexuality. Is there a teenager at home? Snake's appearance indicates a profound change within the family structure—a new birth, the death of an elderly parent or relative, or even a move that impacts everyone involved. Again, note the details surrounding the experience.

Creativity: Snake presages new ideas and opportunities in your creative life. You encounter new people who are helpful to you in achieving your goals and you are now able to embrace new, exciting experiences that relate to your creative passions.

Spirituality: Rebirth and resurrection. Your worldview changes dramatically. Embrace it.

Brainstorming

Whenever you become more aware of the messages that a particular animal holds for you, it's enriching to explore your relationship with that animal in depth. Since the three creatures described in this chapter deal with transformation, here are some suggestions for exploration:

Keep a record of your encounters.

You can do this in a journal, on a computer, a PDA, even a notebook you carry around in the car with you. Include the date, time, and place of your encounter. Describe what happened and what was going on in your life at the time. Even if you don't understand the message at the time of the encounter, it will become clear to you over the next few days or weeks.

Trish, for instance, has an affinity for frogs and over the years, had had numerous encounters with these magical creatures. These encounters invariably happen under odd circumstances—indoors instead of outside—and she is forced to pay attention. Usually, the appearance of the frog means that within the next day or two, she will receive news that is, in some way, transformative. Whether the news is going to be positive or negative depends on the situation surrounding the frog's appearance.

In August 1997, Trish and her family returned home from a trip. In the family room, they discovered that one of the frogs in her collection had gotten knocked off the top of the TV and shattered, probably when one of the cats jumped onto the shelf. But there was also a dead frog in the middle of the family room.

Because these frog events occurred in the *family room,* she felt they foretold events that would impact the entire family. Since one frog was *shattered* and the other was *dead,* she felt they portended trauma, illness, or death to someone close to the family.

The next morning, Trish's husband, Rob, heard that his father was dying. He left for Minnesota and was able to be with his family when his father passed away.

The news with frogs, though, isn't always bad. One morning in February of 2003, Rob announced that there was a beautiful tree frog in the bathroom. The obvious question, how it had gotten into a windowless bathroom, is one they don't ask anymore. Everyone rushed into the bathroom to get the frog outside before one of the cats found it. Since this frog was especially cute (a Cuban tree frog) and everyone was so delighted to find it, they associated it with good news.

That evening, Trish learned that one of her novels had been nominated for the Edgar Allan Poe award given out each year by the Mystery Writers of America.

Start your own list of meanings for particular animals.

Perhaps your experiences with butterflies, frogs, and snakes don't have anything at all to do with transformation. Fine. Then give these encounters a category, research the animals, their habitats and habits.

In South Florida, there's a butterfly preserve called Butterfly World. Here, you can spend as many hours as you want, strolling through magnificent gardens filled with numerous species of butterflies. Employees are on hand to explain the quirks and habits of particular species. For a nominal price, you can buy a little jar that contains a butterfly chrysalis and take it home to watch the butterfly emerge. Is there something similar to Butterfly World in your community?

Maintain an open mind.

This quality is especially important when it comes to snakes. Most people either like them or feel repulsed by them. But if Snake enters your life—or your dreams—it behooves you to explore this reptile's habits and behaviors.

One way to do this is to visit your local zoo. Observe the snakes. Talk to the people who handle them. Take notes, pictures, videos. And if the spirit moves you, find a snake to keep as a pet!

Honoring Your Animal

There are many ways to honor an animal with whom you've had an encounter, but one of the most effective is through educating others.

Let's say you've had an encounter with Snake, a creature that often evokes strong, negative emotions in people. Instead of getting on your soap box and pummeling others with your views, teach through example. Work with snakes. Give talks at elementary schools. Put up a website. Find books that discuss snakes in a positive way.

One summer day in 1997, Trish's cat came running into the house with a snake in her mouth. She deposited it in the middle of the living room floor and then did what cats always do, sat back on her haunches, waiting for it to move so that she could pounce on it. Trish, on her way to the kitchen for a cup of coffee, saw the snake—and froze.

It looked like a coral snake, but she knew it might be a harmless snake. She couldn't remember the rhyme that would tell her which one it was. Fear had wiped her memory clean. She ran over to her cat, grabbed her and the other two cats, who had crept in for a look, and put them in her office. She shouted for Rob, who came running in with a broom, but he couldn't remember the rhyme, either. Was it *red touch black killed Jack?* The snake clearly had red, yellow, and black rings. But what was touching what?

They got on the Internet, the snake still coiled on their living room rug, and found a picture of a coral snake—and the rhyming jingle: *Red and yellow kills a fellow.* If the red and yellow rings touched each other, it was a coral snake.

On this snake, the red and yellow didn't touch. It was a king snake.

Rob got the snake into a paper bag and took it outside.

Did the experience teach Trish not to be afraid of snakes? No. The sight of a snake in your living room, even if it's harmless, is horrifying. But it did teach her that fear blocks information that can prove useful and that snakes, like any animal, deserve our respect.

4

Courtship, Sexuality, Romance, and Love

HORSE, SWAN

Every species of animal has its own courtship and mating rituals. Some species are promiscuous, others are devoted. Some mate for a season and others mate for life. But do animals actually fall in love?

This area is highly controversial. "…Our highest esteem is accorded romantic love, which is considered the most suspect to ascribe to animals," write Jeffrey Moussaieff Masson and Susan McCarthy in their ground-breaking book, *When Elephants Weep: The Emotional Lives of Animals*. The authors point out that romantic love is considered to be so rarefied that many people don't believe that animals are capable of feeling it.

The butterfly fish of Hawaii, for example, form lasting pairs. But does that mean they love each other? Well, if these fish were people, we would say that of course they do! Konrad Lorentz, in his book *The Year of the Greylag Goose*, tells a story about two greylag geese whose love for each other was evident when the female of the pair was killed by a fox. The gander, Ado, remained close to her partially eaten body in the nest and over the ensuing days, his eyes became sunken, he hung his head, and generally moped around. He was mourning. Since he refused to defend himself against attacks by other geese, his status in the flock fell. This story, though, has a happy ending. A year after the death of his mate, Ado met another goose.

Coyotes, which generally are considered to be wily tricksters and aren't particularly liked by people, form lasting pairs. Coyote pairs have been observed hunting together, forming howling duets, engaged in complex displays of touching and licking, and curling up together after mating. As Masson and McCarthy note, "This looks a lot like romantic love. Whatever distinctions can be made between the love of two people and the love of two animals, the essence frequently seems the same."

Chickens also feel love for each other. In his marvelous book, *The Pig Who Sang to the Moon,* Jeffrey Moussaieff Masson tells a wonderful story about a hen found at a city dump in California. She was an older chicken who didn't have much left of her upper or lower beak, the result of a debeaking—a practice followed on chicken "farms." Mary, as the hen came to be called, was rescued by a woman who worked at an animal sanctuary. Soon the chicken became close to a young rooster named Notorious Boy.

"They spent all their time together, hardly interacting with other birds. It was a kind of love, though not sexual," Masson writes. These two were so inseparable that they lazed in the sun together and even slept close to each other at night. During the winter, Notorious Boy "draped his wing over Mary to protect her from the wind and rain, just as a mother hen would protect her chicks."

If we saw such behavior between humans, wouldn't we call this love?

Just as we have certain rituals and rules that are followed during courtship and romance, animals also have certain rituals. Some are simple, involving noises and body behaviors, others are vastly complex. Domestic house cats howl and hiss at each other, dogs sniff and lick each other, elephants bellow, female moths release pheromones, a scent that attracts male moths, and horses whinny, paw, and curl their lips in an odd way. But none of these rituals necessarily point to romantic love; these behaviors seem to be largely instinctual, not much different than the man or woman who is out on the prowl for the evening.

HORSE

Myths, Folklore, Legends

Perhaps the most famous horse in mythology is Pegasus. This great, white winged horse was born from the blood of Medusa when she was decapitated by Perseus. Shortly after its birth, Pegasus was taken by Athena to Mount Helicon to be reared by the muses. One day, the muses began to sing and the mountain, filled with the ecstasy of the music, rose to the heavens until Pegasus kicked his hooves and stopped the mountain's upward progress. A fountain of water rushed forth, called the Fountain of Hippocrene, which became sacred to the muses. The birth of both wine and art allegedly occurred when Pegasus's hooves unleashed this sacred spring.

Bellerophon, prince of Corinth, wanted desperately to ride Pegasus, but the winged horse always avoided capture. Athena eventually sent a dream to Bellerophon, instructing him on how to capture Pegasus and also gave him a golden bridle which would tame the horse. Not long afterward, Bellerophon rode Pegasus when he slayed Chimera, a hybrid monster that breathed fire, and also when he attacked the Amazons.

But Bellerophon wanted to be more than a prince or a king. He sought nothing less than godhood and tried to ride Pegasus to Mount Olympus. Pegasus threw him and was eventually rewarded with spending the rest of his days on Mount Olympus. He is memorialized in the heavens with his own constellation. Not bad for a creature born of blood.

The centaur, half-man and half-horse, is also well known in mythology and in astrology as the zodiacal symbol for Sagittarius. The scoop on the centaur seems to be divided. On the one hand it's considered to be barbaric— a rabble rouser with a ferocious appetite for wine and sex. On the other hand, it's considered to be wise, a quality embodied in Chiron and Pholus.

In C.S. Lewis's series *The Chronicles of Narnia* centaurs are depicted as star-gazers who tell the future by the stars. This could be one of the reasons why Sagittarius rules astrology. Lewis portrays them as wise creatures that are undyingly loyal.

The unicorn is the most magical of horse creatures in mythology. It has the body of a white horse and one straight horn on its forehead. It has appeared in the legends and art of India, China, Islam, and medieval Europe, where it was associated with virginity and with Christ. In modern American fiction, Peter Beagle's classic, *The Last Unicorn,* portrays unicorns as a magical race of creatures whose horn can confer immortality.

Horses and immortality are a prevalent motif in many traditions. Abraxas, for example, is the name of one of the four immortal horses of the god Helios. Aithon was one of the fire-breathing steeds of Ares, the Roman god of war. Notos was the god of the south wind, who in the shape of a horse drew the chariot of Zeus. The Trojan-Hippoi were the twelve immortal horses owned by the king of Troy.

In modern times, look at books and movies like *The Horse Whisperer,* a story in which the horse ultimately acts a healer because of the depth of the love two humans have for a particular horse.

Horses have such a rich tradition in mythology, folklore, and even in fairy tales, that it's difficult to say that the horse belongs in only one category. We chose the horse for this particular category because of its obvious connection with strength and freedom. In the Animals at a Glance section, its relationship with other categories is noted.

Facts and Trivia

About twenty million years ago, horses were the first of the ungulates or hoofed animals that adapted to running on the tips of their toes across the grassy plains. They are distinguished from the other animals in this group by the number of their toes and the ways in which they digest the cellulose content of plant cell walls.

All equines—which include zebras, donkeys, and several subspecies like the Asiatic ass—are grazers and all are social creatures. The horses are the largest of the equines, weighing up to 1,500 pounds, with the males and females just about equal in terms of weight. The domestication of the horse was a crucial turning point in human cultural development. It provided man with a means not only to carry goods, but to travel greater distances more quickly and also a new way to fight wars. What chance, after all, did a foot soldier army have against an army on horseback?

Domesticated horses that have been set free or which have escaped now exist in feral populations on all six continents. But all horses, whether they're wild or domesticated, exhibit highly ritualized behaviors related to courtship and mating. Mating usually takes place in the spring, when the longer daylight hours stimulate hormones that prepare the horses mentally and physically for breeding. When mares are ready to mate, they emit pheromones from their flanks and around their tails. The stallion can detect them up to a mile away and when he picks up the scent, the courtship dance begins.

The stallion moves toward the mare with his neck arched, his head tossing and tail raised. He may circle or follow her, making squealing and nickering sounds. He sniffs and nibbles at her sides, flanks, and around her tail. His upper lip curls over his nostrils so that her scent becomes trapped in his nostrils. Through a special olfactory organ, he is then able to measure her readiness for breeding.

The actual act is over in less than a minute.

Significance

Key Words: Sexuality, power and endurance, spirituality, ritual, strength, groups

The Big Picture: You may be encountering difficult circumstances in your life. If so, you're able to get through this challenging time through the strength and power of your own personality, but with a little help from your friends.

You experience renewed confidence and energy. You may be able to regain a sense of power through working with groups. Any projects that you're involved in will reach fruition in about eleven months.

The context in which your horse experience occurs is important. If you deal daily with horses, then the divinatory meaning may be more intimately connected with how a particular horse interacts with you. Take note of the horse's color, movement or non-movement, and whether it's hostile or friendly.

If you dream of a horse, then you probably need a lot more freedom in your life than you currently have.

Romance: Powerful sexual attraction to someone. The chemistry is perfect. You may meet this person within a group to which you belong or some sort of group endeavor that you attend. You'll be courted aggressively and seduced in an honest, straightforward way—that is, you'll both know exactly what's going on, but it won't be verbalized. Sexually, this relationship is apt to be extremely powerful.

Finances: Your finances are about to improve significantly and quickly. Listen closely to your instincts when it comes to investments and purchases. Events are moving swiftly, so it's necessary to remain alert, aware. If you get involved in a group investment plan—IRAs, Keoghs, even a group stock investment venture where money is pooled—continue to diversify.

Work/Career: Know your opponent. Don't be broadsided. Be informed not only about your competition, but about the market. You work well with a team, but your heart lies with self-employment or with a job that provides you with a lot of freedom. No time clocks for you.

Health: If you've been ill, Horse usually bodes for excellent improvement. If you're healthy, then chances are you're entering a period where you feel "as strong as a horse." Freedom is paramount to your good health. If you have any health issues, they may revolve around digestive problems. Your diet is important at this time.

Family: Timing is crucial. If your family has earned your trust, your loyalty is forever. For a woman, Horse indicates that you're the head of the household.

You may have an extended family—friends, relatives, a group that shares your passions and interests—that is as important to you as blood bonds.

Creativity: You need freedom to delve into the wells of your own creativity. You need to get out and see things, to travel to various cultures and countries and absorb whatever you can. You may find that your creative voice is strongest when you rise early. Sunrise speaks to you.

Spirituality: You should explore your spiritual beliefs and worldviews through groups. Right now, going it alone won't get you as far as working with like-minded individuals.

SWAN

Myths, Folklore, Legends

One of the most beloved fairy tales is *The Swan Princess*. There are many variations on this fairy tale, but the basics don't change. A young princess and a young prince are brought together as children and fall in love. Shortly after they announce their engagement, an evil sorcerer kidnaps the princess and turns her into a beautiful swan. The only time she can return to human form is when she stands in the moonlight under the sorcerer's castle.

In mythology, the swan is a symbol shared by at least two gods. She was often a symbol for Venus, the goddess of love, romance, and the arts, but she's also representative of Apollo, the Greek god of music. Even though swans don't sing in the way that we think of birds singing, there's a belief that they sing as they are dying, which may be where the term "swan song" originated.

The swan also has its own constellation, Cygnus. According to some myths, Queen Cassiopeia supposedly kept Swan as a pet. Other versions say that the swan was actually Cionus, son of Neptune, who was smothered by Achilles. To save his son, Neptune immortalized Cionus as a swan. Cygnus, also called the Northern Cross, is easily spotted in the summer sky, thus its association in divination with the season of summer.

Among the Druids, swans represented the transition of the soul from life to death. One belief held in Scotland says that when three swans are sighted flying together, it's an omen that a national disaster is imminent.

Facts and Trivia

One of the most breathtaking experiences is to see a swan on a placid lake. The bird's majesty and grace is equaled only by its size—it's the largest of the water fowl.

The seven species of swan are found on every continent except Africa and Antarctica, with four of them found in the U.S. The black swan is most common in Australia, particularly across the wetland habitats to the south. The white mute swan, native to central Asia, has been raised in a semi-domesticated state since the time of the ancient Greeks.

In England, all mute swans are owned, by law, by the Crown, a law that dates back to the twelfth century. It's believed that Richard the Lion Heart brought the first swans to England from Cyprus after the third crusade. Not too surprisingly, swans used to grace the dinner tables of kings and queens—not as guests, but as the main course!

The name of the mute swan came about because of the widely held belief that it loses its voice at maturity. The mute isn't actually voiceless—most swans make a hissing noise—but the belief underscores the notion of strength through silence.

Among most species of swans, the birds are ready to mate around eighteen months of age and can raise several broods in succession. Both parents care for the young. Field biologists have confirmed the belief that swans mate for love and are absolute paragons of marital devotion. When the mate dies, the survivor usually doesn't bond again.

The average male swan isn't as gentle as it looks. It's able to break an adult man's arm with one beat of its wings. Swans can be ill-tempered birds, particularly if they are protecting their young.

Swan certainly fits into more than one category, but we felt that its capacity for long-term pairing made it an ideal example for this chapter. Its other categories are noted in the Quick Peeks section in Part Three.

Significance

Key Words: Grace, beauty, fidelity, love, protection of children and family, monogamy

The Big Picture: You're in love or about to fall in love and this relationship could be one between soul mates. It doesn't guarantee that everything from here on will unfold with utter smoothness. But as long as you both recognize a past-life connection, you're in a much stronger position for lifetime commitment. In terms of timing, look to summer.

When you have an experience with a swan, take note of the context. What were you doing at the time? What was the swan doing? What happened in your interaction? Was the bird friendly, hostile, or simply indifferent? Also note the weather, the temperature of the air, and the color of the swan. All of these traits help define the divinatory meaning of the encounter.

When you dream of the swan, it may be necessary for you to be more protective of your children, if you have any, or of your "creative children." It could also portend that love is on the way.

Romance: Soul mates reunite. If you're already involved in a committed relationship, then your feelings for each other deepen considerably. The person you meet may be the gorgeous, silent type, but could have a bit of a nasty temper. The attraction between you and this other person initially may be simply a recognition, a profound sense of déjà vu.

Finances: If you're not already involved in the family business, you may be soon. Your parents may either loan you the money you need or give it to you as a gift. This could include a down payment on a home, car, or for college. It's possible that you will help your parents or other relatives financially.

Work/Career: When Swan comes into you life, you may be working for a small, family-owned business. The business could belong to your family or to a family of complete strangers, but either way, the atmosphere will provide the love and protection you need at this point in your life. Or, you may be considering opening your own business and hiring your family members. Either way, the point is to work in an atmosphere that is small and familiar.

Health: The happier you are, the healthier you are. The same could be said of all of us, but for you the connection is crucial. Try not to bottle up anger. Allow yourself to express it freely, but without harm to others. Express it, release it, then move on. If you don't do this, it's sure to eat away at you.

Family: When Swan appears in your life, it could be that you need to pay more attention to what is going on with your mate and children. Or, you may be feeling more protective toward them than usual. Your home is important to you at this time. It's what makes you feel most secure. Go ahead and indulge your need to nest, to secure, to bond.

Creativity: It's important that you find your creative niche and pursue it. Don't listen to the naysayers who are quick to tell you you'll never make a living doing what you love. It all begins with your belief in yourself.

Spirituality: At this time, your deepest spiritual experiences revolve around your significant other and your children. Your family lies at the heart of your spiritual exploration.

Brainstorming

If you have an experience with a horse, there are a number of things you can do to enhance and deepen the connection, which in turn attracts more experiences. Here are some suggestions:

Meditation and Dreams.

If you meditate, call upon Horse to lead you where you need to go. You might have an image of a horse or a horse figurine or statue somewhere nearby. Before you fall to sleep at night, visualize a horse and request a dream in which Horse will guide you toward knowledge or illumination that you need in some area of your life.

When Trish's daughter, Megan, was very young, she was fascinated by unicorns. She loved watching cartoons and paging through picture books that featured unicorns. She loved hearing stories about them and was especially fascinated that her dad had written an Indiana Jones book called *The Unicorn's Legacy* and used to ply him with endless questions about the power of unicorns. Trish and Rob eventually wallpapered her room in a unicorn motif.

During one period of Megan's life, she used to wake from nightmares in which she was being chased by ugly creatures. Trish and Rob told her that the next time she had a nightmare like that, she should conjure one of the unicorns on her wallpaper and ask the unicorn to whisk her to safety.

During one nightmare, she came awake within the dream and called on a unicorn for help. The next morning, she rushed out into the kitchen, announcing that she had ridden a unicorn to safety!

Not surprisingly, Megan is now an avid rider.

Rent horse movies, read horse books.

If you haven't seen *The Horse Whisperer*, then do yourself a favor and rent the DVD or video. Another excellent horse movie is *The Black Stallion*, and then, of course, the perennial classic, *Black Beauty*.

The book version of *The Horse Whisperer* is every bit as good as the movie. Another classic: *The Last Unicorn*.

Seek out horses.

Don't limit your knowledge of horses to books, movies, dreams, or meditation. Get out and meet a horse. Take riding lessons. Find a stable where you can hang out or a pasture where you can while away a few hours observing horses. Talk to people who work with or own horses.

If Swan has entered your life, you may have to be a bit more innovative. Perhaps there's a bird sanctuary in your community where you can volunteer. Or if you live near a lake in an area that swans frequent, take nature walks to observe them in their habitats. Visit a zoo that has swans. Poke around on the Internet to research these magnificent birds.

One woman we know who was fascinated with swans honored the bird through artwork and poetry. Her home office is filled with photograph montages of swans. And on a rainy night, rent *The Swan Princess* and travel back through the magic of your own childhood.

Honoring Your Animal

Every pet owner we know honors their animal companion in some way. Our dogs have special beds where they sleep at night. Our cats get catnip toys and special treats. Our birds ride around on our shoulders and live in comfortable habitats. When we go away, our animals often have pet sitters come in to look after them. We collect dog and cat and bird totems—figurines, carvings, artistic reminders of the special places our animals have in our lives. We speak up when we see instances of abuse or neglect.

But how do you honor a horse or a swan? In much the same way.

One day at a local barn, a stubborn horse refused to do what it was supposed to do during a lesson. Maybe it wasn't feeling well or didn't like the rider or was just feeling plain ornery. Whatever the reason, the teacher told the student to get off the horse and she promptly got on the horse and began beating it with a crop, jerking on the reins, forcing the horse to do what she wanted.

The mothers who witnessed this were so appalled at what was happening, they shouted at the teacher to stop. "He has to learn," she shouted back, and the abuse continued until one of the mothers marched out into the ring and screamed, "Enough!"

The teacher stopped, shocked at their response, and the mothers withdrew their kids permanently from the classes.

Sometimes, honoring your animal means that you stand up for what you believe and intervene.

5

Messengers

OWL, DRAGONFLY

In J.K. Rowling's Harry Potter books, mail is delivered to the young wizards and witches by owls. They soar through the windows of the castle while the kids are in the Hogwarts' dining hall and drop off letters for their respective owners. Harry's snowy owl, Hedwig, is certainly patient enough, enduring long summers in his cage at the home of the Durleys, the relatives with whom Harry lives when he isn't at school. Hedwig has a personality all his own, and is unerringly loyal to Harry.

Rowling's enchanting books feature all sorts of animal messengers— from owls to large tropical birds to mythological creatures like the phoenix to animals that are purely imaginary. In the *Chamber of Secrets*, the phoenix, which is reborn periodically within its own ashes, saves Harry's life by healing him of the snakebite through its magical, healing tears.

Any animal can act as a messenger, but in mystical traditions creatures that fly seem to play the messenger role frequently. Birds, in particular, are considered in many traditions to be the messengers of departed souls or to be the souls themselves, returning to help the living along their path through life. Old wive's tales and superstitions abound with stories that the death of a bird in or near your home portends the passing of a loved one. If a bird taps at your window, superstition says it's an omen of impending death for one of the occupants of the house.

Rather than dismissing these superstitions as nonsense, it's to your benefit to remain open-minded. See how these experiences play out in your own life. It may be that the bird tapping at your window is alerting you to something positive that is coming your way.

Crows and ravens have long been symbols of occult knowledge and power, of wisdom, and of war. Crows are generally viewed as symbolic of bad tidings, but whether they mean that for you depends on how you view them. In the popular folklore of Great Britain, ravens are considered to be omens of power and wisdom. This belief is so embedded in superstition that it's considered to be terrible luck if ravens leave the Tower of London, so their wings have been clipped.

Swallows are greatly maligned in popular lore. In some traditions, a close encounter with a swallow can portend anything from a severe illness to death by murder. But that doesn't mean it's necessarily the case for *you*. If you've had great experiences with swallows throughout your life, then there's no reason to believe that Swallow is a harbinger of terrible things.

The dove is considered in most cultures to symbolize love, peace, and harmony. White doves are particularly auspicious; in Christian tradition, they symbolize the holy spirit of Christ. The robin and the bluebird also enjoy positive reputations as messengers; they supposedly bring luck, fun, and passion. The woodpecker is another lucky winner in the messenger category; if one is seen near your home, you can expect good news and favorable experiences.

The bird that surpasses all others in terms of joy and luck, though, is the eagle. It's considered to be a symbol of strength, good fortune, and a helper to humanity since the days of the Roman empire.

But birds aren't the only kinds of messengers. In the movie *Dragonfly*, Kevin Costner plays a physician who has lost his pregnant wife and whose grief nearly overwhelms him. His wife, who was also a physician, was killed in a bus accident in South America, while tending to native children. She had a special connection to dragonflies and in the aftermath of her death, Costner experiences a number of strange synchronicities that involve these ephemeral creatures and which ultimately lead him to finding his son, born just as his wife was dying.

This movie is intriguing precisely because the theme of the dragonfly as a messenger is not only carried throughout the story, but becomes the vehicle for Costner's journey back into himself. The dragonfly is Costner's lucky charm. This symbol for luck was also evident in medieval Japan, where the dragonfly was revered for its accuracy and strength and was sometimes carried as a symbol of luck by Samurai warriors.

The bat is another intriguing messenger and its reputation is nothing to write home about. Throughout mythology and history, the bat has been considered to be an omen of death, unlucky, even downright evil. However, it seems to have some redeeming occult qualities. The heart of a bat, when dried and turned to powder, can supposedly stop bullets or prevent you from bleeding to death. If you wash your face in bat's blood, you can suddenly see in the dark. But the bat is also about intuition, dreams, and the hidden, which is why we put it in Chapter Nine.

OWL

Myths, Folklore, Legends

Across time, borders, and cultures, the mythology and folklore about owls seems to be one of extremes. They are either harbingers of death or of healing, of unspeakable evil or of wisdom. They are symbolic of both white and black magic, are helpful or harmful, revered or despised. They have been associated with weather phenomena and with esoteric and mystical occurrences. Regardless of your color, race, or spiritual beliefs, you can't be indifferent to the significance of Owl.

The most common meanings of owls in mystical traditions is that they are wise (maybe it's how they look) and that they move freely between the world of the living and the world of the dead, equally at home in both. Zulus believe the owl is the sorcerer's bird. Among Australian Aborigines, owls are considered to be the souls of women—and bats the souls of men. In Celtic tradition, the owl was the symbol of the underworld. In Ireland, it's believed that if an owl flies into your home, it should be killed immediately, otherwise it will take the luck of the house away with it. In Madagascar, it's believed that owls join witches to dance on the graves of the dead. In Morocco, the cry of an owl supposedly kills infants.

Owls are also considered to be powerful symbols of protection and healing. In ancient Babylon, owl amulets protected women during childbirth. The Inuit consider the owl to be a source of guidance and help. In Mongolia, owl skins are hung up to ward off evil; in Peru, owls are considered to be strong shamanic medicine; and in Siberia, the owl is considered to be a helpful spirit.

Since the owl is a nocturnal animal, it's divinatory meaning is often connected to the night, to what is hidden or secretive.

Facts and Trivia

Two families of owls exist—the Tytonidae or barn owls, with eighteen known species, and the Strigidae, with nearly two hundred species. Most owls are nocturnal birds of prey and are found on every continent except Antarctica.

Most owls have large eyes, forward-facing to increase binocular vision, and highly specialized to allow them to see in very dim light. Barn owls have exceptional hearing and are able to hunt and catch prey in complete darkness guided only by sound. The shape of the head and the external feathering around the face allows sound to reach the owl's ears in a unique way. By turning its head, an owl can locate a low sound—like that of a rodent eating—with extreme precision.

The female owl is usually larger than the male. As a general rule, she and her partner are monogamous during the breeding season. A species called "little owls" however, are monogamous for an entire year, and pairs of tawny owls are faithful to each other for life. This is why owls also fall under the "loyalty and devotion" category.

Although owls are always territorial, this trait is especially evident during the breeding season. They're especially aggressive and courageous in defending their nests and the surrounding territory, even against other owls and birds. Tawny owls, which are less migratory than other kinds of owls, defend their territories throughout the year and often defend their offspring from the previous breeding season. Their attacks can be particularly vicious if the intruder stands up to them. If the intruder is human, they don't hesitate to use their talons and beaks on the person's face and eyes. There are documented cases of people losing an eye from a tawny owl attack.

Owls lay between one and thirteen eggs, with three or four as the average. The eggs are laid over a period of days, just as they are with ducks and some other species of birds, so the hatching is staggered. This means the chicks born last are usually the weakest, and they often starve or are killed by their siblings.

Owls are extremely vocal. In addition to hoots, owls also whistle, screech, scream, purr, snort, chitter, hiss, and click. Hoots are usually associated with courting and clicks with threats.

Significance

Key Words: Messenger, wisdom, healing, insight, clairvoyance, life/death, loyalty/devotion

The Big Picture: Something is hidden from you. But the owl's appearance in your life indicates that you're able to see the truth behind what is hidden in a situation, relationship, or event. It may be time for you to delve more deeply into a study of the occult, shamanism, reincarnation, and communication with the dead. If the owl appears while someone you know is ill, it may be warning you that the person is getting ready to cross over.

The owl can also signal a change in your sleep cycle or be alerting you that you are more creative during the night. In terms of your personal health, the owl encourages you to seek alternative therapies and help from alternative practitioners. If you have a persistent health problem, you may want to consider having a regression to find out if the problem stems from a past life.

As always, consider the context of your experience with an owl. The weather, the time of day or night, and the owl's actions are all significant.

Romance: If you're not involved with anyone right now, you will be shortly. The relationship is likely to be emotionally intense and the other person may be something of a loner who is involved or interested in metaphysics. If you're involved now, then the relationship may move to the next level. You'll know intuitively what's going on. Communication is important to you in relationships and it's important that the other person also communicates his or her feelings. Past-life connections may be involved.

Finances: By summer, you could be earning money through psychic or metaphysical work. Work with your dreams for guidance about finances and request specific dreams that will alert you to new opportunities.

Work/Career: You vigorously defend your territory and are something of a predator when it comes to the hierarchy at work. However, you don't have the full picture and it would be to your advantage to hone your own skills to get ahead professionally.

Health: Have you considered alternative therapies? Homeopathy, acupuncture, even yoga or tai chi may be what you need right now. It's also possible that on an emotional level, you need roots, a place that you can call home. You may need to change your sleep cycle—or at least experiment with different sleep cycles. Seek guidance from your dreams related to your general health.

Family: Someone in your family—children or a mate—needs your support and protection now. Give it freely without expecting anything in return.

Creativity: You're entering a period in your life when your most creative time is at night. This doesn't mean you have to stay up all night to be creative. But you may want to set aside several hours at night, after the rest of the family is asleep, to do what you love. Your creative adrenaline will flow most easily in the evening.

Spirituality: Consider taking workshops in shamanism. You have a talent for altered states of consciousness, alternative healing techniques, and metaphysical practices. If someone you love has recently passed away, that person's death may be the trigger for your spiritual journey.

DRAGONFLY

Myths, Folklore, Legends

These magnificent insects have inhabited the planet for three hundred million years, long before the first dinosaur appeared. They—and the closely related damselfly—have a rich tradition in mythology and folklore.

Thanks to its needle-like appearance, it has been referred to in mythology and folklore as the "devil's darner," the "water witch," and the "snake doctor." In European and early-American lore, a dragonfly would sew a person's eyes and ears shut as they slept. In Swedish lore, dragonflies were called "Blindsticka" or "Blind Stingers," and supposedly enjoyed poking out human eyes. In other myths, the dragonfly was credited with being in league with the devil, who used it to weigh people's souls.

In Great Britain, the dragonflies were once considered to be dangerous and evil and were called "horse-stingers" because they were always seen darting around horses.

Not exactly a great reputation, this dragonfly. Fortunately, there are other sides to the story.

The same Swedes who referred to dragonflies in such disparaging terms, also recognized them as sacred animals. Among members of one Swedish cult, the dragonfly symbolized the love goddess Freya.

The ancient Japanese were great admirers of dragonflies. Farmers believed the dragonfly was the spirit of the rice plant and that its presence in the field portended a good harvest. The dragonfly later became the symbol for victory in battle and was honored as an emblem of the emperor. An old name for Japan—Akitsu-shimu—means Dragonfly Island.

The Zuni regard the dragonfly as a messenger of the gods and a savior of people. The Mimbres of the American Southwest regarded the dragonfly as the symbol of life and painted it on ceremonial pottery. The Navajos believe the dragonfly is symbolic of water purity.

Even though we have included dragonfly under the messenger category, it also belongs under *luck* and *prosperity* and *transformation*.

Facts and Trivia

Dragonflies are living fossils, part of the most ancient group of insects on the planet. In prehistoric times, they were much larger, with wing spans of more than thirty inches. Today's version has a wingspan of about five and a half inches.

Both the dragonfly and the damselfly have four wings, long, very thin abdomens, and three pairs of legs. The dragonfly, a fast, powerful flyer, can reach speeds up to thirty miles an hour, whereas the damselfly mostly just flutters around. The dragonfly's eyes touch at the top of his head, where the damselfly's eyes are widespread. When at rest, the dragonfly holds his wings out to each side, as if proudly showing them off, and the damselfly holds hers closer to her body.

More than sixty percent of the dragonfly's total body weight is composed of flight muscles. Its aeronautical abilities are fascinating to watch and some of its maneuvers—ninety degree turns, for example—are so quick it's difficult to track with the naked eye. He can hover, fly backward, maneuvering his four wings independently of each other. He can even eat while he flies. He has a monstrous appetite and his eating begins in the larva stage, when he floats on the surface of water or on the surface of water plants.

In this stage, where he spends most of his life (six months to four years), he will eat virtually anything that crosses his path—including mosquito larva. During the larva stage, he's completely dependent on water and breathes through gills. At this stage, he's one of the favorite foods for frogs and fish.

At some point, the dragonfly larva climbs onto a reed or plant, sheds his final layer of skin, and emerges as an adult, much as a butterfly transforms from the caterpillar stage. He flies off and returns to the pond only when he's prepared to mate, which is what the last part of his life is all about. That's when the air show starts and it's also when the dragonfly possesses its most vibrant colors. He rarely rests and can even mate in the air.

Dragonflies have incredible eyes. They're composed of a complex system of honeycomb lenses that produce multiple images that the little dragonfly brain somehow converts into a comprehensible image. Some of the larger dragonflies have nearly thirty thousand lenses in their eyes. Although they prefer to hunt during the day, they can see very well in the dark.

Significance

Key Words: Messenger, transformation, joy and luck, insight, clairvoyance, change

The Big Picture: When the dragonfly crosses your path, you can count on a message arriving soon. More often than not, the news is good. You need to use your intuitive insight to understand a situation or relationship. Some facet of your life is about to go through a transformation. Ultimately, all transformations help us to fulfill our potential.

It's time to find your creative passion and pursue it. You have the physical, emotional, and spiritual stamina to succeed at whatever you do.

Note the circumstances of your dragonfly experience. If, for example, the dragonfly flits by in front of your car while you're driving, then the meaning is much different than seeing a dragonfly while you're sitting next to a pond in the woods. It could be that your "vehicle" of change or transformation is much closer than you imagine. If you see multiple dragon-flies in an area outside of their natural habitat, expect good luck very soon!

Romance: A dragonfly may portend a sexually active time in your life. If you're a woman, this could be a good time to try to get pregnant. If you're male, you may be contemplating starting a family or having another child. Just be sure that you have pierced your own illusions and understand what truly motivates you. It's also possible that you're being courted—or will do some courting—in a flashy, flamboyant way.

Finances: The check you're expecting is in the mail. It may not be a huge check, but be grateful for it. It's a good time to brainstorm with friends or a significant other for ways to make additional income. Don't be fooled by opportunities wrapped in flashy packaging; the bottom line is what matters.

Work/Career: A career change is in the offing. You've been hoping for an opportunity to break away from what you're doing, and it's just around the corner. You may have to make a sharp ninety degree turn in your life to seize the opportunity, but you're up to the task. Decide what you want to do, then go for it.

Health: Develop a deeper awareness about what you eat. Is it nutritionally sound? Have you been eating on the run? Your body will tolerate junk food only so long before it rebels. Start shopping at a health food store. Seek advice from a nutritionist or holistic practitioner about diet. You may benefit from eating smaller, more frequent meals.

Family: Get out there with your loved ones and do something that's pure fun. Forget work, forget professional concerns, forget the corporate climb. Discover the Zen of the moment.

Creativity: Your creativity is innate. But now you'll learn through experience just how diverse and multidimensional creativity really is. Make time in your life for your creative passions.

Spirituality: You're shedding your worldview and spiritual beliefs and are moving toward something entirely new. The transformation may be scary at times, but the end result will allow you to better fulfill your enormous potential.

Brainstorming

Once you've had an experience with an owl or a dragonfly, you can deepen your connection with the animal by consciously working with the energy the owl and the dragonfly represent. The more conscious you are, the more likely it is that you'll attract more experiences. It's like Carl Jung's observation about synchronicities: Once you become aware of synchronicities operating in your life, they suddenly seem to happen more frequently. Here are some suggestions you may want to consider:

Keep a journal of your experiences.

This should be done regardless of what kind of animal experience you have. But for messengers, it's especially important. By recording details such as time, date, location, and the specifics of the experience, you build a frame of reference. Once the message is obvious to you, it's possible to go back to the particular entry and add additional notes.

There are many other messenger animals—check out Part Three for our entries—and if you have experiences with any of them, record these, too. Some people seem to attract messenger animals, perhaps because some part of their unconscious needs to be reminded of their connection with life's deeper rhythms. Or perhaps they're simply at a juncture in their lives where they need advance information. You may go through a period like this and it's important for your own growth and awareness to have a record of these events.

Explore divination techniques.

For some people, an experience with a messenger animal triggers an interest in other divination techniques—the tarot, the *I Ching*, runes, palmistry, astrology. Experiment and find the right divination technique for you.

Create an environment for your messenger.

If your favorite messenger is a dragonfly, then build a pond in your backyard that has plants and flowers that attract dragonflies. If owls frequent your life, then make sure they have a place in your yard that welcomes them. You get the idea here, right? *We* have encroached on *their* worlds. The least we can do in return is to honor their presence in our lives by creating environments that are to their liking.

Honoring Your Animal

During the late 1980s, Trish and her husband, Rob, led tours for travel writers to the Peruvian Amazon. The tour began in Miami, where the writers boarded a flight for Bogota, Colombia. After an overnight in Bogota, the group left the next morning for Leticia, Columbia, a strange, dusty border town at the edge of the Amazon River, wedged between Peru and Brazil. From there, they boarded an old boat—formerly a vessel that hauled rubber back and forth across the Atlantic. The boat was a sister of the one used in the movie *Fitzcarraldo*—i.e., not the QEII.

The decks on the boat were open to the humid Amazon air and perfect for sightseeing as the vessel churned its way slowly through the Peruvian Amazon, 350 miles upriver to Iquitos, Peru. It was ideal for spotting wildlife along the river—monkeys, parrots, toucans, ocelots, river dolphins the color of bubble gum.

Every day, the boat anchored in the river and the writers took side trips in skiffs to the small, primitive villages. Here, they traded *gringo* trinkets—lipstick, balloons, chewing gum, cigarettes—for hand carved spears, blow guns, and then, one day, an owl.

The owl was kept on a chain on a young boy's shoulder. Its feathers had lost their sheen, its eyes seemed dull and listless, and it seemed to have lost its will to live. Trish asked the boy if he would trade the owl for something and the kid eagerly nodded and asked if there were any transistor radios. They settled the deal with a little transistor from Target and the owl took up residence on the open deck.

For the first twenty-four hours or so, it didn't do much of anything except watch. Trish tried to feed it, but the owl wasn't interested. Then the writers all went fishing for piranha and someone brought the owl a live fish—suddenly its interest in life was revived.

One guy on the boat called Trish a "mush head" about the owl in particular and about animals in general and kept referring to anthropomorphism, the term that scientists and lay people love to toss around because it gives them an excuse to view animals as merely a low cog in the food chain. He never contributed a coherent travel piece on the Amazon. In fact, he didn't contribute much of anything to that trip except annoyance. As it turned out, he was terrified of the owl.

During those three days on the boat, the owl began to take a deep interest in where it was, in its surroundings. At night, it sat on its perch, alert, vigilant, those magnificent eyes moving with incredible dexterity, that gorgeous head swiveling nearly a hundred and eighty degrees, those amazing ears catching every sound, every nuance. By the third day, it permitted Trish and Rob to touch its head, to stroke it.

The owl's final destination was the jungle camp in Iquitos owned by Paul Wright, the American expatriate who also owned and operated the boat. It joined a veritable zoo of rescued and exotic birds that roamed freely around the camp, greeting passengers with songs long gone from the civilized world.

There are many ways to honor the messengers in your life and you don't have to go to the Amazon to do it. Many cities have bird sanctuaries or bird rescue organizations that cry out for volunteers. If you don't have time to spare, but have money to burn, then consider a donation. There are also eco-tours that specialize in bird watching, zoos that boast impressive owl populations, and yes, there are plenty of barns and pastures and backyards where owls can be welcomed.

One woman with a great affinity for owls took a recorder with her to a rural area and at dusk, recorded the hoots and clicks of barn owls. She then mixed the sounds into her favorite meditation and yoga tapes. A teenage boy who enjoyed photography and loved owls created a portfolio of photos of owls and decorated his room with the pictures.

Regardless of how you honor messengers, the expression is as much about you as it is about the animal. Be creative. Let your imagination soar!

6

Loyalty, Devotion, and Family Bonds

DOG, ELEPHANT

hen we created this category, we were thinking of animals that are loyal and devoted to humans. This trait is certainly part of the equation. But as we talked about which animals to describe in depth for this chapter, we realized that loyalty and devotion should also include animals that are loyal and devoted to their mates or to other animals, as well as family bonds.

More than ninety percent of the bird species are monogamous and some of them form lifelong bonds, certainly one of the human definitions of loyalty and devotion. Biologist Bernard Heinrich, an expert on ravens, believes that ravens fall in love. "Since ravens have long-term mates, I suspect they fall in love like us, simply because some internal reward is required to maintain a long-term pair bond," he writes in *Mind of the Raven*. They have been known to hold bills while courting, often sleep next to each other in the nest, and they preen and play with each other.

Loyalty and devotion among animals aren't limited just to mates any more than human loyalty is. "It is common for horses to make friends with other animals such as goats," write Jeffrey Moussaieff Masson and Susan

McCarthy in *When Elephants Weep*. "Accounts of racehorses who mope and do not run well when separated from their goat friends are numerous. These goats may well be the equivalent of pets."

Anyone who owns a dog knows all about loyalty and devotion. Man's best friend, after all, is the companion that greets you at the door with that tail wagging a mile a minute, who covers your face in kisses even when you don't deserve it, and who gives new meaning to the corny line in *Love Story* about never having to say you're sorry. A dog usually loves you no matter what. But what about the dog who shares the house with pets of other species?

At Trish's house, Jessie the golden retriever shares her space with three cats, a dusky conure, a black and white mouse, and a hermit crab. Since her first day at the house, she and the cats have gotten along. But it wasn't until Trish and her family moved that they understood the kinds of bonds that existed among this odd menagerie.

The cats had gone to the vet for two days while everyone moved and the day they were brought home, Jessie ran to the door and greeted each one of them, her tail wagging, her licks profuse and happy. The cats, in turn, touched noses with her, rubbed up against her, and licked her. The humans stood around, gaping, understanding for the first time that Jessie considered the cats to be her extended family and that the cats apparently regarded her as one of their own. The male cat, Whiskers, is a wanderer, and on nights when he refuses to answer Trish's call, she brings Jessie outside with her and asks her to find Whiskers. Jessie walks up and down the block, sniffing around, not seeming to look for anything, and Whiskers invariably shows up and rubs up against her in greeting.

Even the bird seems to understand that Jessie is okay. She rides on Jessie's back and, with a bit of human involvement, has learned to drop doggie treats in Jessie's mouth. The cats don't bother the bird, the bird has learned to call them scaredy cats, and the mouse and hermit crab sit serenely in their respective habitats, trying to make sense of it all.

Some years ago, Millie had a Boston Terrier mix, a silver poodle, and a domestic white short-haired cat named Peter. Peter had gotten himself into trouble and had wandered off into the woods for a couple of days. Millie, worried because she knew that he needed medical attention, asked the two dogs to go out and find the cat and bring him home. Several hours later, they appeared in the yard, the dogs flanking the cat. This unlikely trio remained fast friends for years, another instance of an extended family.

Taz was a pit bull, but had been raised on love and was a loyal, loving pet. He belonged to Donna, but stayed with Gay, Donna's mother, while she worked. For several days while swimming in the pool, Taz refused to allow Gay to swim into deep water. She was totally perplexed until, while driving to the store after swimming one afternoon, she had a heart attack and wrecked her car. She was shaken but uninjured. After her doctor's diagnosis, Gay understood Taz and what he was trying to relay. Had Gay been in the pool when she'd had the attack, she would have drowned.

Brunie, a German Shepherd, was a gift to Frank because she refused to accept her new owner, Woody. Brunie stuck to Frank like glue—accompanying him to the barn, the pig sty, or after the cows. No one was allowed on the property without Frank telling Brunie it was all right. They had been together three years when Frank and his wife bought a new home in town. Three weeks after they moved, Brunie started howling one night for no apparent reason. The next day, Frank became ill and died of a heart attack.

When Frank didn't return home, Brunie went to the farm looking for him. She spent several days going back and forth from the farm to the new home. When she couldn't find her best friend, she refused to eat and crawled up under the porch and died of starvation and grief.

Josh is another story that illustrates a dog's loyalty to the people it loves. Josh was born in the living room late in July. Millie, the owner, refused to dock the tail of this poodle because she wanted to enjoy seeing it wag. He was black, with a white muzzle, and grew up in a household with Millie's cat. Millie was never quite sure whether Josh thought of himself as a dog or as a cat.

Millie gave Josh to her mother, Florence, to keep her company during the day while Millie was working. The three of them became a special trio. As Florence began to lose her hearing, Josh realized she was having problems and began to be her helper in many ways. When the phone would ring, Josh would gently grab her hand with his teeth and take her to the phone. If there were someone at the door, this amazing little fellow would run back and forth until she followed him to the door. When Florence became bed-ridden after breaking her hip, Josh stayed beside her bed and guarded her.

Josh and Florence died within a few days of each other. Both of them died of congestive heart failure. Florence was 100 years old and Josh was 16 in human years, the dog equivalent of 112.

The family bond among certain species like foxes, wolves, and coyotes is well documented. But, quite often, animals who live in groups form friendly bonds with others members of the group. "A monkey kept alone will work for the reward of seeing other monkeys, just as a hungry one will work to get food," write Masson and McCarthy. "The animals in a social group have relationships with each other, some of which are affectionate."

They point out that lionesses babysit for each other. This is similar to the dolphin nursemaids, who help other dolphins give birth and take care of the babies after they are born. It's as if these social relationships function in much the same way that they do for people. Who's to say we humans have the final say on emotions? As Nobel–prize winner Konrad Lorentz once said, "The quickest way to learn the language of a species is to do so as a social partner."

In a sense, we become social partners with the animals who grace our lives, however briefly. Through this interaction, we deepen our understanding of ourselves and our place in the grander scheme of things.

In selecting the animals to highlight for this chapter, we finally settled on two. The first, the dog, is associated with unflinching loyalty to man. Our second example, the elephant, has exceptionally strong extended family bonds. Even though most of us probably won't have an encounter with an elephant outside of a zoo, these majestic creatures have much to teach us about loyalty, devotion, and family bonds.

DOG

Myths, Folklore, Legends

Dogs have a special place not only in folklore and mythology, but in contemporary literature, where novelists often use them as metaphors for ideas about the spiritual realm.

In *Harry Potter and the Sorcerer's Stone,* a three-headed dog, probably based on Cerberus, the three-headed dog of Greek mythology, guards a coveted secret. In Ian McEwan's haunting novel, *Black Dogs,* the ferocious beasts are a metaphor for the evil in the world. In Dean Koontz's novel, *Watchers,* a pair of golden retrievers represent both the paragon of evil and the paragon of purity and goodness. In Stephen King's novel, *Cujo,* a St. Bernard that is a family pet contracts rabies and is transformed, through no fault of his own, into a monster of terrifying proportions and becomes the vehicle of transformation for the female protagonist.

But modern writers are simply using the mythology and folklore that has existed for millennia about dogs. In shamanic lore, hounds guard the entrance to the land of the dead. In ancient Egypt, the dog—depicted as the jackal-headed Anubis—was associated with the underworld. At that time, Anubis was connected to the star Sirius, the brightest star in the sky, known as the "Dog Star." Statues of Anubis graced the entrances to Egyptian temples. In Finnish, British, Celtic, Roman, and Welsh traditions, dogs play similar roles. In the ninth century, there was a divination rite involving dogs that entailed foretelling of the future by chewing on the flesh of dogs (and pigs and cats). All of these traditions may explain why dogs are said to possess second sight and seem to sense when a loved one is about to die or has passed on.

In Greek legends and myths, we find references to dogs as helpers to humans. Xanthippus, the father of Pericles, supposedly owned a dog that swam by his side when the Athenians were forced to abandon their city. The dog was buried beside his master at a site called Cynossema, the dog's grave. Alexander the Great allegedly founded and named a city, Peritas, in memory of his dog.

In ancient China, dog trainers were held in high esteem and kennel masters controlled large groups of dogs. In Chinese culture, the "Fu Dog" is associated with bringing happiness and good fortune. In Zoroastrianism, a religion introduced in ancient Persia nearly three thousand years ago, dogs were revered. One of the seven volumes of the *Zend Avesta*, the sacred books of that religion, is devoted to the care and breeding of dogs.

The dog was revered in Babylonia. It is the sign of the Phoenician physician Gala and is associated with Artemis of Greek myth, Diana of Roman myth. Australian Aboriginals consider the dog an essential companion and some African tribes consider the dog a culture hero.

Dogs also make an appearance in Norse myth: Odin has two dogs that are messengers. The Iroquois sacrificed white dogs as intermediaries to the gods. In China, the Buddhist Lion Dog is the guardian of the law.

The Greek Diogenes and his followers were called "Cynics" from the Greek word for dog, because they were moral watchdogs.

When a dog howls in the night it is said to be an omen of death.

Dogs are thought to be aware of the presence of ghosts and their barking or howling is often the first warning of supernatural occurrences. Packs of ghostly hounds have been recorded all over Britain. In Northern England, there is a myth of an animal named Barguest, who appears as a big black dog with large eyes and feet that leave no prints. In Scotland, a strange dog coming to the house means a new friendship.

Facts and Trivia

The dog is the oldest domestic animal and dates back to Paleolithic times, when man tamed dogs to help track game. But the dog as we know it first emerged in Eurasia about 13,000 years ago, a descendant of the small gray wolf.

The tallest dogs are the Irish wolfhound and the Great Dane. The smallest dogs are the Chihuahua, the Yorkshire terrier, and the toy poodle. The St. Bernard is the heaviest dog. The three smartest dogs are the border collie, poodle, and the golden retriever. There are 701 types of pure breed dogs.

Contrary to popular opinion, dogs aren't color blind. They can see color, but it isn't as vivid as what a man can see. Their sight isn't as good as ours, but they can hear sounds that are 250 yards away. Where we hear sound waves vibrating at frequencies up to 20,000 times a second, dogs hear sound waves of 35,000 vibrations per second. The dog's sense of smell far exceeds that of man. Where man has 5 million smelling cells, dogs have as many as 220 million.

Significance

Key Words: Loyalty, devotion, unconditional love, clairvoyance, metaphysical knowledge, companionship, guardian, protector, helper, nurturing parent

The Big Picture: Companionship and loyalty are important to you. You're a social person who seeks meaningful connections and relationships with others. It may be time for you to develop or trust your intuition. In a mate, you're seeking a long-term commitment in which you and your significant other can give and receive without fear or restriction. If you're a parent, you tend to your children's emotional, physical, and spiritual needs with great care and diligence.

If you own a dog or dogs, the type of dog will tell you a great deal about your individual energy. If your dog is playful and loves to tease, then the message may be that you need to become more playful and childlike and to balance work with relaxation. Look for the metaphoric meaning in your pets' activities and personalities and how it relates to your situation.

If a stray appears on your doorstep, then it's time for you to embody the qualities that dog represents.

Romance: Whether you're involved or not, your love life is about to pick up. It's possible that you'll meet the love of your life within sixty days. You're not interested in a purely sexual relationship, but in sharing your life with someone whose interests and passions are similar to yours.

Finances: Trust your intuition about investments. If you would like to earn your living working with dogs and other animals, then it's possible to do so now. Be alert for opportunities and seize them when they present themselves. Sixty days is a good time frame.

Work/Career: You're entering a period when you're going to be "working like a dog." You may assume more than your share of responsibility, but you do it out of love for what you're doing. Your loyalty to the job will be well-compensated.

Health: When the dog appears in your life, you're being reminded that love is the greatest healer. Just as you may be healing someone else's spirit, that person may be healing yours. Be open to alternative therapies. Consider meditation as a means of developing your intuitive insight and yoga as a way to increase your flexibility. The downward dog, a particularly challenging yoga posture, is one that you should strive to master. As yoga practitioners say, "You're only as healthy as your spine is flexible."

Family: Someone in your family circle needs extra care and attention now. A child is in need of a greater sense of protection and more love. In fact, if you don't have a dog, maybe it's time you bought one for the family!

Creativity: You pursue your creative passions with a "dogged determination" and the deepest belief in your abilities. A mentor helps you find the right venue for creative expression—or you serve that purpose for someone else.

Spirituality: Love is the most powerful force in the universe. The dog, after all, loves unconditionally.

ELEPHANT

Myths, Folklore, Legends

As the largest living land mammal, elephants are abundantly evident in mythology and folklore. Buddha's mother supposedly dreamed that a white elephant, one of the most sacred animals in myth, entered her womb. In India, the elephant was considered to be the vehicle of kings and to this day, there is a celebration in southwestern India called the Great Elephant that commemorates the animal's power and majesty.

When King Porus of India fought Alexander the Great in 326 B.C., he was wounded from numerous arrows and his elephant supposedly saved his life. The beast left the battlefield, lowered his master gently to the ground, and then dislodged the arrows from Porus's body. Alexander was so astounded by this act of compassion that he commemorated Porus and his elephant on a coin that depicted the king and his elephant, with Alexander and his horse beside them. But Porus and the elephant are much larger. The actual coin is now in the British museum.

In Indian temple architecture, elephants appear to be holding up the temples. The Indian god Ganesh, who has a human body and the head of an elephant, is worshipped as a sign of well-being and prosperity.

Facts and Trivia

Elephants live and travel in groups that are usually blood-related and headed by a matriarch, an older female elephant. There can be anywhere from six to twenty elephants in a band. Male elephant babies stay with their mothers until they're grown and then join the male herd. Sometimes, the bands of males travel with the matriarch and the herd of females and their young.

Thanks to the work of researchers and animal behaviorists like Cynthia Moss, who leads an elephant research project in Kenya, and writers like Jeffrey

Masson and Susan McCarthy, we now have information about the emotional bonds among elephants. When a member of the herd dies, elephants display what can only be termed grief and sorrow and seem to have certain rituals surrounding death. Cynthia Moss reports on the behavior of an elephant herd circling a dead companion, then turning outward and finally turning inward again, toward the dead elephant. The elephants then tear out branches and leaves from surrounding vegetation and drop them over their dead companion.

Masson and McCarthy relate a story that came from Cynthia Moss concerning an elephant jawbone that Moss brought to her camp so that she could determine its age. The dead elephant's family traveled through the camp several weeks after its death and showed great interest in the jawbone. "Long after the others had moved on, the elephant's seven-year-old calf stayed behind, touching the jaw and turning it over with his feet and trunk." One can only agree with Moss's conclusion that the calf was somehow reminded of his mother—perhaps remembering the contours of her face. "He felt her there."

Elephants are known to help other members of the herd. If an elephant is hurt, the herd will slow down so that it can keep up. Older calves often help younger siblings. Elephants have also been observed to weep. In 1955, an elephant trainer named George Lewis was training a group of elephants for a circus act. One of the elephants, Sadie, couldn't understand what they required of her and ran out of the ring.

"We brought her back and began to punish her for being so stupid," Lewis wrote in *Elephant Tramp*. The punishment probably involved being beaten on the side of the head with a stick. Sadie, who was already lying down, began to sob, tears streaming from her eyes. Lewis and his trainers were so shocked they immediately knelt beside her and began caressing her and talking to her. She subsequently learned the trick and Lewis never punished her again.

We often talk about man's inhumanity to man, but what about man's inhumanity to animals? Until we learn to treat animals with compassion and the dignity they deserve, we will continue to treat each other shamefully, waging war in the name of peace, abusing our children and spouses, conducting tests and torture experiments on living things so that we can "understand them better." As Masson and McCarthy note, "Other than humans, no animal runs torture experiments on other animals."

Significance

Key Words: Loyalty, devotion, family-oriented, ancient power, royalty, heightened sexuality, joy, awareness of the cycle of life and death, strength

The Big Picture: Since elephants are known to be playful and to demonstrate great joy, these qualities are definitely part of the larger picture when one of these majestic creatures comes into your life. Your personal and family relationships may take on these qualities. A new relationship may be founded on joy and playfulness. However, the elephant also embodies great sexual power, so any romantic relationship you're involved in may be highly sexual as well.

The elephant also fits under the category we've called power. It isn't just physical strength and power, but an ancient, mystical power as well. It could be that people you meet during this time are those with whom you share past-life connections. You'll recognize these individuals intuitively and may begin to have dreams that are actual past-life memories about places and events where you've known these people.

Romance: You enter a period of heightened sexuality and passionate, intense sexual experiences. The chemistry may be rooted in past lives you've shared with this person. Twenty-two months from now, your love life will have undergone a complete transformation. Bonds of deep loyalty are formed.

Finances: You are challenged to earn money in a way that is aligned with your deeper beliefs. Animal conservation and awareness is one possibility, psychic work is another. You're in a position now to empower your employees and to empower yourself as well. Use this window of opportunity to maximize your potential.

Work/Career: You may be shouldering burdens and responsibilities right now, but take heart. It pays off in the long run. Just be sure that you slot time for some R and R and that you get adequate sleep. Friends and group associations are helpful professionally.

Health: You're in a good period health-wise. To maintain it, join a gym and try to lift weights a couple of times a week. A daily discipline like yoga or tai-chi would be beneficial, too. You may want to try a vegetarian diet for a couple of weeks just to see if you feel any differently.

Family: Your family and loved ones are highlighted now. If you're trying to get pregnant, the news is positive. You may find, too, that your family is growing because a relative or a close friend moves in for awhile. You offer help freely to those you love.

Creativity: You're in a place of great power and sensitivity and everything you need to do your creative work is available to you. Use this time wisely and don't be afraid to embrace the unknown in your creative work.

Spirituality: Past-life associations prevail during this time. Your connection to your higher self is especially strong and information is available to you through dreams, in meditation, and through synchronous experiences.

Brainstorming

If you have an experience with a dog or an elephant, pay very close attention to the details. This category is deeply revealing about who you are—your capacity for compassion, for giving and receiving love, and your ability to love unconditionally.

Unless you work for a game preserve, a zoo, or live on the African plains, you're more likely to have an experience in waking life with a dog rather than an elephant. However, if you do have an encounter with an elephant in your waking life or in a dream, here are some suggestions for deepening the connection between you and this magnificent animal:

Books.

At the top of the list for reading material is *When Elephants Weep,* a phenomenal book that explores the emotional lives of animals. The stories about elephants are unforgettable and will permanently alter the way you think and feel about them.

Avoid circuses.

It seems almost un-American to say it, but circuses have always struck us as a gross and cruel form of entertainment. To watch elephants rear up, dance, and do tricks at the whim of their trainers, to see them on thick, short chains, to see them standing listless—where's the entertainment in that? Where's the humanity?

Don't buy ivory products.

In the wild, elephants are hunted for their tusks, which are harvested and then sold. They eventually appear in third world marketplaces as carvings or are used in aphrodisiacs. The importation of ivory into the U.S. has been banned for a long time, but if you travel outside the country, don't buy ivory.

Education.

Educate your children about elephants—their habitats, their behaviors, their emotions. Tell them stories that make elephants come alive as beings every bit as intelligent as man. Find books and movies about elephants that you and your kids can enjoy together.

Give to wildlife organizations.

Provide charitable contributions to organizations that protect elephants and their habitat.

What about dogs? Some of the same activities apply—books, movies, educating yourself and others about canines in general or a particular breed. But here are some other possibilities to consider:

Adopt a dog from the Humane Society or a dog rescue organization.

There are so many dogs in need of adoption that before you go to a breeder, take a look at the Humane Society or your local animal control shelter. Consider adopting a dog from an organization that euthanizes animals.

If you're looking for a pedigree dog, then check out the Internet for rescue organizations for the breed you want. There are rescue organizations for practically every breed of dog—from greyhounds to golden retrievers to papillons. These organizations tend to have stringent requirements for adoptions. They do home visits, assess the household to make sure that it meets the requirements of the breed, and approach the adoption of a dog as a lifetime commitment to the animal.

Avoid puppy mills.

A puppy mill is any place that breeds dogs the way cattle or chickens are bred for food—the female dog is impregnated almost continually so there's a steady supply of pups.

Speak up about instances of abuse.

If you witness an instance of abuse, report it to the authorities. A friend of ours, Vivian Ortiz, who lives near Savannah, was on her way to work one day and saw an emaciated dog chained to a post in a front yard. The dog had no water, no food, and the temperature that day was soaring. The dog's chain collar was so tight on its neck that the skin had grown over it.

Vivian not only reported it to authorities, she pressed charges, had the dog removed from the home, and took it to her vet. The chain collar was so deeply embedded in the dog's neck that the vet had to remove it surgically. She later testified against the dog's former owner in court and ended up adopting the dog. Jackson, as he's now called, is still skittish around men, but lives happily with Vivian and another dog, and two cats.

There are other forms of abuse that people perpetrate against dogs that are more subtle and perhaps even as damaging. One woman we know buys expensive dogs (and other animals), keeps them until she gets bored with them—six or seven months—then gives them away or has them put down. In one instance, a dog she gave away now lives in the same neighborhood, and it still runs back to this woman's yard to whine and bark at the fence, as though asking what went wrong.

It's important to speak up.

Honoring Your Animal

Whether you have an experience with a dog, elephant, or some other animal that falls in this category (see Part Three), there are many ways to honor the animal. If your animal is wild, then consider taking a photographic tour of the area where the animal lives. If your animal is more common or domesticated, like the dog, then consider volunteering at one of the dog rescue organizations. If the dog is your animal companion, then here are some other suggestions:

Show your love for your animal companion on a daily basis.

All too often we get caught up in the daily frenzy of life and forget that our pets need to know that we love them.

Include your dog in family outings.

This can be something as small as taking your dog in the car with you when you go to the grocery store or something as big as taking your dog camping. Many national parks allow dogs as long as they are leashed.

Meditate with your dog.

Yes, this sounds a bit strange. But really, it amounts to sitting quietly with your dog in a familiar setting, perhaps outdoors if the weather allows it, and entering into some sort of communion with your companion. This is also an excellent way to begin telepathic communication between you and your dog.

7

Creativity and Self Expression

SPIDER, SPARROW

Every animal is inherently creative, with unique evolutionary adaptations that allows it the best opportunities for survival. This made it challenging to select two animals to discuss in depth for this chapter.

Even at a cursory glance, there are many animals whose creativity is evident in what they do. Spiders spin exquisite webs. Hummingbirds, butterflies and bees pollinate the earth. Beavers create amazing architectural wonders in their dams. Cranes grace our marshes and wetlands. Parrots learn how to speak. Humpback whales sing. Pumas are incredible athletes, able to leap fifteen to twenty feet straight up. A chimpanzee is able to lift six times its body weight. Rabbits ensure their survival by being prolific. Gray whales migrate 26,000 miles a year. Dolphins are known for their altruistic acts toward humans.

It could be argued, naturally, that these activities and qualities are instinctual and don't have anything to do with creativity. But if that's what you actually believe, then you probably doubt any connection exists between your encounters with animals and the state of your life, so you won't get very much out of this book. On the other hand, if you believe that all of life—and everything and everyone in it—is inherently creative and interconnected, then you won't have a problem with the two animals we selected for this chapter: the spider and the sparrow.

SPIDER

Myths, Folklore, Legends

Spider Woman is a prevalent myth in Native American creation mythology and lore. Native Americans believed that the threads of Spider Woman's web connect the world of humans and the world of spirit; that she weaves the web of life; and that she brings the people sunlight. This theme is artfully explored in a movie called *Kiss of the Spider Woman,* for which William Hurt won an Oscar.

Among the Navajo, Spider Woman and Spider Man are holy people who taught their tribe how to weave. Among the Pueblos, Spider Woman is an important mythic being. The Hopi consider her to be a creator who helped their people during their emergence into this world and created the moon, has the power to give and take life, and is connected to hunting and agriculture. The Cherokees believe that she brought their people sun and fire, and taught them pottery, weaving, and how to make ceremonial blessings. For the Tewa and Kiwa tribes, Spider Woman is responsible for bringing fire.

In Africa, the spider plays a similar role, but is often depicted as Spider Man, who plays a role in creation and saving life, bringing wisdom, fire, even food and water from heaven during droughts. In many myths about spiders, the spindle is the axis on which the world revolves. Plato, for example, had a vision of the goddess Ananke, spinning the universe: The sun, moon, and planets were her spindle's whorls and souls moved through the webs of time and fate that she wove, traveling between life and death and rebirth.

Some of the most interesting myths about spiders are urban legends. One that we've heard for decades is how spiders favor nesting in hair that is heavily sprayed and teased. Another involves the daddy long legs—that they are one of the most venomous spiders, but that their fangs are too short to bite humans. How this urban myth got started is anyone's guess, but it's common enough so that kids often repeat it as though it were fact.

Another fascinating urban legend involves the brown widow spider in Southern California. In February 2003, specimens of this non-native spider were discovered as part of a survey being conducted by the Los Angeles County Museum of Natural History. The subsequent media attention conveyed the false impression that the brown widow was a new danger in Southern California. While the spider is venomous, it doesn't inject enough venom to kill. What's especially interesting about this urban legend is that it's the kind of fodder that fuels Hollywood horror movies like *Arachnophobia*.

Then there's the modern day version of folklore: *Spiderman*. The story was first introduced decades ago by Marvel Comics and later became a successful movie starring Tobey Maguire. The storyline is simple: A high school student, Peter Parker, is bitten by an irradiated spider and develops arachnid-like powers. Like other superhero characters, Parker decides to use his astonishing abilities to protect humanity.

Facts and Trivia

Spiders are among the oldest creatures on the planet. They first appeared 400 million years ago, nearly 200 million years before the first dinosaurs. There are about 35,000 named spider species worldwide, with some 3,000 species just in North America.

Spiders, like insects, are invertebrates but they have only two main body parts rather than the three parts that insects have. The spider's body consists of a combined head and thorax called the cephalothorax and the abdomen. The cephalothorax has eyes, mouthparts, and four pairs of legs. These characteristics are shared by ticks, mites, and scorpions, all of which are classified as *Arachnida*. Spiders, however, have their own classification within this group—*Araneae*—because they have a slender waist or pedicel that separates the cephalothorax from the abdomen. They're covered by a tough exoskeleton that has sensory hairs growing from the skin.

Spiders have claws at the end of each leg, a rather bizarre sight when you see them for the first time. A web-building spider typically has three claws that help it cling to its web, and its natural body oils prevent it from getting stuck. Spiders have eight eyes, with one pair acting as the main eyes; these have a small field of vision and high resolution. The secondary eyes allow the spider to detect the difference between light and dark.

Tarantulas are the largest spiders. They don't spin webs and usually hide during the day in burrows or dark holes, which they line with silk. A female tarantula in captivity can live as long as thirty-five years. In the movie *Arachnophobia,* the spider in the opening scene that crawls across a man's pillow while he's sleeping in his tent (and subsequently bites him) is a tarantula. The Goliath tarantula *(Theraphosa blondi),* the largest spider in the world, is the size of a tennis ball, with legs that can be as long as ten inches. *Arachnophobia* was filmed near Angel Falls, in Venezuela, where the Goliath lives; the local Piaroa Indians frequently eat it.

Wolf spiders, like tarantulas, don't spin webs. They live and hunt on the ground and dig burrows. Female wolf spiders carry their babies on their backs, a point that Jeffrey Masson and Susan McCarthy speculate about in *When Elephants Weep.* "What if it was discovered that when a mother wolf spider sees young spiders, her body is flooded with a hormone whose presence is associated with feelings of love in higher animals? Would that be evidence that the spider loves her young?"

While we don't usually associate spiders with parental love or any other kind of love, just ask any small child who has read *Charlotte's Web* or seen the movie whether a spider like Charlotte is loveable!

Web-building spiders have spinnerets, a special kind of gland in their abdomens that produce a protein that's squeezed out as a liquid. As soon as the liquid comes into contact with air, it hardens. Two types of silk are produced—a dry silk that doesn't stretch and a sticky silk that does. The latter is what's used to catch insects.

Worldwide, there are about a dozen very venomous spiders. The best known in North America is probably the black widow spider, followed by the brown recluse spider. The black widow's venom is neurotoxic, which means that it affects the nervous system and not just the area around the bite. The recluse's venom is necrotic, meaning that it affects the tissues around the bite. Australia boasts between fifty and a hundred venomous spiders, with the Sydney funnel spider as one of the most venomous. The Brazilian huntsman allegedly has the most toxic venom of any living spider, with just .006 milligrams of the stuff enough to kill a mouse.

Significance

Key Words: Creativity, self-expression, camouflage, self-protection

The Big Picture: When Spider enters your life, be sure to notice the details. Who, what, where, and when, are good places to start. Who, if anyone, were you with? What happened, and what kind of spider was it? Where did the encounter happen? The significance of an experience will be different if you walked into a spider's web than if you woke up and found a spider crawling up your chest. When refers to the time of day or night, the season, the environmental conditions, and anything else that might provide insight to the experience.

If you're bitten, then the meaning of the experience is obviously vastly different than if Spider simply drops onto your desk as you're working.

Romance: If you're single or uncommitted, then you're about to meet someone who will share your creative interests and passions. The relationship could evolve into a creative partnership. If you're committed or married, then the relationship may be taking a decidedly creative turn. There's good chemistry here.

Finances: You're called upon to be more creative in the way you earn money, or it may be time to start earning your daily bread by doing what you love most. Or, it could be a combination of both. The nuances lie in details: the kind of spider, where the experience occurred, what you were doing at the time.

Work/Career: At some point during the next six months, you may change jobs or careers to do something more in line with your creative interests.

Be alert for synchronicities that will guide you toward your new direction. It's a time to tie up loose ends, put the past to rest, and get on with what you really want to achieve.

Health: The web you spin with your thoughts, emotions, and beliefs has a direct bearing on your health. If you have a nagging health problem, look for the metaphor. Stiff joints, for instance, may alert you to a rigid belief in some area of your life. Toxic emotions like bitterness and anger can lodge in your body unless you release the emotions and understand their source.

Family: It's time to spend time with your family, doing things that everyone enjoys. Have your kids express their thoughts and desires about what they would like to do as a family. Whether you're planning a weekend or a long vacation, get everyone involved.

Creativity: Explore the vastness of your own creativity. Research Jungian archetypes, ancient patterns, primal energies. Books can be helpful in this regard, but the real meat lies within your own unconscious. Find the times of the day or night when you feel most creative. Set aside time each day to indulge your creative interests. If you want to pursue your creative interests as a career, then set goals that are reasonable and work toward those goals each day. But remember: True creativity is about how you live your daily life.

Spirituality: Creativity is one path toward the exploration of your spiritual beliefs. The two are intimately connected.

SPARROW

Myths, Folklore, Legends

According to one popular tale, the sparrow was present at the crucifixion of Christ. It kept crying out, *He is alive,* which prolonged Christ's torture. The bird's punishment for this was to have its legs bound, which is why it now hops around. But in another version of this story, its presence throughout the crucifixion made it a symbol of triumph after suffering.

In a Japanese fairy tale called *A Tongue-Cut Sparrow,* an old man came across a wounded sparrow and brought it to his house to care for it. He nursed the sparrow back to health and the bird became quite tame. One day, while the old man was out, the bird ate starch made by the man's wife. Being a crabby sort of woman, she got angry about it and cut the sparrow's tongue. Wounded again, it flew away.

When the old man got home and discovered the sparrow was gone, he set out to find it. He traveled through the mountains and finally arrived at the hidden kingdom of the sparrow. The birds gave him a warm welcome and before he returned home, presented him with two wrapped gifts, one large, one small. He selected the smaller one because he didn't think he could carry the larger one back through the mountains.

At home, he opened the gift. It was filled with gold. His wife, already a crabby old woman, now showed that she was also greedy. She scolded him for not selecting the larger box, which she figured held even more gold. She got him to tell her where the kingdom of the sparrow was located and went there herself. The sparrows tried to welcome her just as they had welcomed her husband, but she rebuked them. She told them she simply wanted the other present—the larger gift.

This box was heavy, and she had to rest as she trekked back home. When she opened the box, monsters emerged and assaulted her.

The moral? Well, our interpretation is that sparrows remember kindness, but aren't immune to getting even when the situation calls for it!

In Hindu myth, the sparrow is symbolic of fertility. In ancient Rome, the sparrow was sacred to Venus.

Some ancient people believed the sparrow symbolized the gods of the household and family, so that if one flew into the house, it should be nurtured. Another superstition related to sparrows is that rain is on the way when a group of them chirp in unison.

Facts and Trivia

There are twenty different species of sparrows and all display the opportunistic ability to survive wherever they are.

The song sparrow is extremely adaptable. It's found across a wide geographical range, within many different kinds of climates, and seems to thrive regardless of where it is. Its song can be heard every month of the year and during the day or the night, which is why we've put it in the category of creativity and self-expression. When the weather is cold, the song sparrow can eat nearly five thousand seeds an hour just to maintain its temperature level.

The sparrow can live up to ten years in the wild and more than twice that in captivity. Most sparrows will visit feeders if you put them out, with the white-throat sparrows beating out most of the others and getting the birdseed first. American tree sparrows, which usually live in northern forests, tend to visit feeders only when they're migrating.

House sparrows, contrary to their name, belong to the weaver finch family. They have become pests in recent years, perhaps because they're so adaptable to urban environments, Even so, between 1972 and 1996, it's estimated that their population in the U.K. fell by 64 percent, with the loss of nearly ten million birds.

Significance

Key Words: Adaptability, new opportunities, creativity through music, singing or songwriting

The Big Picture: When Sparrow flies into your life, the next eleven to fourteen days will be crucial to your creative passions. You may be working longer hours at your creative endeavors, but loving every second of it. Like the song sparrow, your joy at doing what you love will spill over into other areas of your life. Pay special attention to the way you communicate—your tone of voice, what you say, how you say it. Be open to all opportunities that come your way now.

Romance: Your creative endeavors attract a partner whose creative interests are in line with your own. A creative partnership could evolve from this romance, and if it does, it will probably happen rather quickly. Once your energies meld, there's just no stopping the momentum!

Finances: New opportunities are headed your way. Some risk may be involved, but you're a survivor precisely because you're willing to take risks and embrace change.

Work/Career: When Sparrow crosses your path, it's time to walk the talk. If you want to work at what you love, then you need to plan ahead: Save your money, set a date when you'll leave the nine to five world for good, and do whatever it takes to make this happen. Trust your higher guidance. Be as flexible as your nature allows and don't dismiss any opportunities, even if they initially seem outlandish or completely off the mark. You can't predict where such opportunities may lead you.

Health: Be attentive to your diet. If you've been thinking about becoming a vegetarian, for instance, then take steps in that direction. If you've been considering a regular exercise routine, then start it today. Your point of power lies in the present. Your satisfaction with your work and all the other areas of your life have a direct bearing on your health.

Family: Have you considered a family-owned business that expresses your collective creativity? Think about it. If it interests you and your loved ones, begin brainstorming on how you can combine your talents and interests. On a personal level, you may have to commit more time to tending to your children and their concerns.

Creativity: You're entering one of the most creative periods of your life. You're finding your creative tempo and voice and may want to experiment with different times of the day and night to create or brainstorm. If possible, try to bring some element of the outdoors into your work area—live plants or a water fountain, for example—and make sure your work area overlooks plants, a garden, or a pool of water. Investigate Feng Shui, the Chinese art of placement. You may need to rearrange the furniture in your work area or use different colors to enhance chi— energy.

Spirituality: Your creative path and your spiritual beliefs are intertwined.

Brainstorming

If either Spider or Sparrow has come into your life (or any of the other creatures that fall in this category), there are activities you can do that will deepen your connection with these animals—and with your own creativity. Here are some suggestions:

Take nature walks.

As any creative person will tell you, a nature walk feeds the soul and brings you closer to the source of your muse. It also enables you to look for spiders and sparrows and observe them in their native habitats. If it's winter, you may have to opt for an indoor aviary or, as with the spider, may have to look in the shadowed corners of your own garage or home.

The creative act.

Watch a spider in the act of creating its web and take photographs of the various stages. Post the photos where you do your creative work. For sparrows, record the songs, then listen to them while you're being creative.

Study other divination techniques.

Divination is an intuitive art and deepens your knowledge of yourself, your creative abilities, and helps you understand how you fit into the larger scheme of things. When you study various techniques after an encounter with an animal associated with creativity, you may find that you catch on to the techniques more easily.

Start with the Medicine Cards. The deck and book will enhance your awareness of the role of animals in your life. Tarot cards and books are readily available, and the meanings of the cards are easy to learn. Other techniques are runes, the *I Ching*, astrology, even regular playing cards. Millie sometimes uses regular playing cards for divination, and employs a system that has evolved over her many years as a psychic.

Movies, Books.

Read or rent *Charlotte's Web*.

Honoring Your Animal

To honor Sparrow, you might create an environment in your yard or around your home that will attract the bird. This facilitates your bird-watching and allows you to observe the bird, photograph it, and sketch it at your own leisure. Or, if you're the adventurous type, take a bird-watching vacation that includes sparrows. There's nothing like firsthand observation to fully appreciate Sparrow's creative gifts.

Visiting an aviary or bird rescue facility can be illuminating and educational. You may notice something about Sparrow that deepens your understanding of your experience with the bird. Birds have aviaries, but what's the spider equivalent? As far as we know, there aren't any facilities devoted exclusively to spiders. However, there are plenty of Internet sites devoted to these creatures. If you google the word "spiders," nearly a million and a half links come up. You can download photographs and information, and even "travel" to the Australian outback and see some of the world's most venomous spiders, and can find out what the experts say.

Probably the most telling way to honor a spider is to not kill those that get into your home. For some people, this may be difficult because spiders, like snakes, trigger powerful emotions. Change places for a moment with the spider. Suppose it were large and you were tiny?

Years ago, Richard Matheson wrote a novel called *The Incredible Shrinking Man,* which subsequently was made into a movie. The premise is simple: A man and a woman are out on their boat one day when it passes through a mysterious fog or mist. The woman is in the cabin as the mist envelops the boat and the man is topside. When the fog passes, he notices shimmering flecks on his chest and thinks nothing of it. Over the course of the next few days and weeks, he begins to shrink.

During one of the final scenes in the movie, when the man is no larger than a straight pin, he fights a spider for food. What is so singularly horrific about this scene isn't the fight; it's how huge the spider is and how tiny the man is. Once you've seen the movie, this scene will spring into your head in its full, glaring terror the next time you feel compelled to step on a spider.

8

Joy, Peace, Luck, and Prosperity

DOVE, HUMMINGBIRD, LADYBUG

These four words represent what most of us strive to achieve in our lives. If we have these four things, then it's likely that we also have happiness, love, good health, and spiritual fulfillment. We chose two birds—the dove and the hummingbird—for detailed descriptions, but there are a surprising number of animals that symbolize at least one of these traits.

Chances are, you owned a piggy bank when you were a kid. Maybe you still own one. So where did that image of a pig as prosperity come from? Why did we have piggy banks instead of, well, dog banks? Or horse banks? Why a pig? In the Chinese zodiac, the pig is associated with wealth, prosperity, and fertility. The pig is a frequent symbol on German beer steins and symbolizes good luck. Among the ancient Greeks, the pig was considered to be sacred because Zeus was suckled by a sow.

Among Hindus, cows are considered to be sacred because they might embody the soul of a loved one who has been reincarnated. Among the Celts, however, cows and cattle were regarded as symbols of wealth and prestige. In ancient Egypt, three goddesses were often depicted as cows and the cow came to symbolize the mother of the pharaoh.

But let's take smaller creatures. In China, the goldfish is thought to be symbolic of prosperity. In Feng Shui, a tank that contains goldfish is believed to attract beneficial energy into the home and to maintain strong psychic and emotional energy. Crickets are among the smallest creatures around, but when one of these little guys graces your life, good luck and prosperity are just around the corner. In China, crickets and grasshoppers were considered to be symbolic of an abundance of good luck. They also represented a fighting spirit.

If you live close to nature or have animal companions, then it's likely you have your own list of animals whose appearance means good luck. For Trish and her family, the appearance of a frog often symbolizes that someone in the family will be hearing good news very soon. For you it may be a mole or a groundhog, a ladybug or a butterfly. As you move through the course of your life, your animal symbols may change as you change. The point is to be aware of the synchronicities in your own life that hint at the underlying connections between events and animals.

DOVE

Myths, Folklore, Legends

Doves seem to be a universal symbol of peace, what Carl Jung would call an archetype. They appear in the art and folklore, religious and spiritual traditions of many cultures.

One popular belief in ancient times was that the dove is the one bird into which the devil can't transform. In Catholicism, the dove has long been a symbol of the Holy Spirit in the Trinity. In the Bible, the dove was the first creature released from the ark by Noah, and when it returned with an olive branch in its beak, it was a signal that the flood had ended.

In Greek myth, the dove was Athena's bird and represented the renewal of life and love and fidelity, so the dove has an association with lovers and romance. At the end of the Olympic games, whose traditions date back to ancient Greece, doves are released to symbolize the spirit of the games.

In ancient Japan, the dove was sacred to the god of war, but a dove with a sword pronounced the end to war. Among the Pueblo Indians, dove feathers were used in prayer sticks, and among other indigenous tribes the dove contains the soul of a lover and to kill one means misfortune.

Doves also have an association with oracles. Alexander is said to have consulted the oracle of Dodona, where the priests interpreted the rustling of leaves and the cooing of doves to inform mortals about the will of the gods. Alchemists believed that the dove was symbolic of sublimation, an alchemical process for purification.

No wonder, then, that in today's world, doves are often found in nursing homes, Alzheimer's facilities, and even hospitals. The soft cooing is found to have a soothing effect on the residents and patients. Because of the dove's association with peace, perhaps its presence speaks to some deep part of the psyche and soothes the transition into death.

Facts and Trivia

Doves and pigeons are blood brothers. The fundamental difference between them lies in their size. Pigeons are generally larger and doves are more delicately built, feed on seeds and fruits, and aren't commonly found on the ledges of Manhattan high rises. When you see old ladies in Central Park tossing peanuts to flocks of birds, the birds are probably pigeons rather than doves.

Yet, both pigeons and doves have that characteristic soft cooing that tends to soothe our frazzled nerves. Most doves are tree-dwelling, but some flock on the ground. Both doves and pigeons produce crop milk when they're breeding, and it's fed to the young. Both species lay one or two eggs and the chicks are cared for by both parents. The kids leave the nest in seven to twenty-eight days. Keep this time frame in mind when you have an experience with a dove.

It's believed that the dodo bird was derived from pigeon-like ancestors that flew to remote islands in the Indian Ocean. It was discovered in 1507 and was extinct less than two hundred years later, the victim of human folly and persecution. Passenger pigeons, which once numbered in the billions, were also hunted to extinction.

In urban America, doves are easy prey for domestic cats. If your cat brings home a dove, as ours have done, examine the bird for the extent of the injury. If there's an open wound, take it to an aviary vet or try to cleanse the injury with warm water and apply some type of antibiotic salve. Quite often, the thick feathers prevent injuries and the dove you think is badly injured is merely stunned. Keep it warm and safe, make sure it has water and seed, and when it seems to have revived and begins to eat, take it outside and, holding it in the palm of your hands, see if it flies away. If the bird was only stunned, it should take just a few moments for the dove to realize it's now free to leave.

And then ask yourself what this experience was *really* about.

Significance

Key Words: Peace, harmony, calm

The Big Picture: Whether Dove flies into your life or is brought into your life by your cat, the bottom line is the same: Where in your life do you need peace and harmony? It's possible that your partnership or marriage or even your children need more of your attention right now. Dove may be telling you that in the next seven to twenty-eight days, you'll need to carve out time for peace and harmony as a defense against stress. Dove's song reminds you of your connection to the earth and to the collective sea that unites us all.

If you dream of a dove, then you may be entering a period in your life marked by great peace and tranquility.

Romance: Within the next twenty-eight days, you may meet the person who will become the love of your life, your soul mate. If you're already in a committed partnership, then during the next twenty-eight days the relationship is going to evolve to a newer, deeper level. Or, it's possible that you need to pay more attention to your partner and to the relationship.

Finances: Vast improvements are indicated! By trusting your intuition, you enter into a period of peace and harmony where money is concerned. The more abundant you feel, the more positive your thoughts, the greater your chances of success on the financial level. Now, repeat: *I accept abundance in whatever way it comes.*

Work/Career: You may find yourself in a role as peacekeeper or mediator in a dispute or negotiation. Your diplomatic skills at this time are impressive and attract the attention of your boss. A raise or promotion may be in the offing.

Health: Are you processing your experiences at this time? Your digestive system may need some attention. A change of diet may be indicated for awhile or you may want to try eating fresh papaya or taking papaya enzymes to aid in your digestion.

Family: You should spend more quality time with your partner and your children at this time. Perhaps a family vacation or even a long weekend together is indicated. Or, it may be that you and your loved ones will be involved in some type of peace rally, athletic competition, or spiritual path together.

Creativity: You and your partner join forces in a creative venture. If you've always wanted to own your own business or to work for yourself, then now is the time to commit and make it happen. Things will move more quickly with a partner than they would if you ventured off on your own. If you have musical abilities that you have always wanted to develop and explore, now is the time to begin.

Spirituality: You and a partner become involved in a joint exploration of a spiritual belief system. Your intuitive connection to each other at this time is especially strong.

HUMMINGBIRD

Myths, Folklore, Legends

Among indigenous people, hummingbirds were thought to possess great magical and healing powers. In the American Southwest, hummingbirds were associated with love and romance, and their feathers were thought to attract love or were added to magical love potions. In Central America, a dead hummingbird may be worn around the neck in a medicine bag to attract love. Or, it can be dried and a few pinches of the powder can be added to a drink of the person whose love is desired.

In folklore, Hummingbird is often associated with long-distance travel. Among the northern Paiute Indians, for instance, it's believed that Hummingbird filled his pants with seeds and began a journey to see what lay beyond the sun. Even though he ate only a single seed a day, he had to turn back when he ran out of food. But the point is that he even attempted the journey!

In one tale, a prince with a fantastic singing voice lived in the middle of a forest. When he sang, animals gathered around him, attracted by the beautiful music. The keeper of the animals, perhaps because he was jealous or just extremely grumpy, didn't like this and killed the prince. Two angels brought him back to earth, but with one change: He was now covered in feathers. The angels had turned him into a hummingbird.

In the Ecuadorian Andes, hummingbirds are believed to represent joy, beauty, the magnificence of creation, and the celebration of life. Outside of the town of Baños, named for its hot mineral baths, there's a hacienda frequented by twenty-seven different types of hummingbirds. They hover from dawn to dusk around the numerous feeders the owners filled with sugar and water.

In the Northwestern U.S. Native American culture, hummingbirds are regarded as messengers and healers and symbolize agility, love, and beauty.

Facts and Trivia

Hummingbirds and swifts are classified as the same family, but this may change in time because the classification has been challenged. Of the 404 species in this classification, which also includes crested swifts, 38 species are listed as endangered.

The 320 species of hummingbirds cover a vast geographical range, from North America to the tip of Tierra del Fuego, from rainforests to the Andes. The average weight is less than a third of an ounce, with the smallest species—the bee hummingbird—weighing in at a tenth of an ounce.

The hummingbird's wings beat twenty-two to seventy-eight times a second, too fast for the human eye to see. When the wings are beating, they emit a humming sound, and are perfectly created to allow the bird to hover while feeding and to execute astonishing aerobatic maneuvers during courtship and territorial chases. It's the only bird that can fly backward.

Its primary food is nectar and its long, needle-like beak is ideally suited to extract it from flowers that are tubular-shaped, like columbine, trumpet creeper, bee-balm, and jewelweed. Hummingbirds need constant access to nectar to fuel their metabolism, which is higher than any other bird's. Some flowers depend solely on hummingbirds for pollination, a clear example of how birds are connected to the biosystem in which they live. If a particular hummingbird becomes extinct, then the flower it pollinates won't be far behind.

The hummingbird breeding season is locked into the local flowering cycle. Once hummingbirds mate, the mother does everything, including building the nest, incubating the eggs, and feeding her young. The nests are intricate, shaped like cups that are held together with plant material and pieces of spider web. Nests are built with great care and each one is unique. These birds don't mate for life, like doves do, and tend to be loners, except when migrating. Every fall, the ruby-throated hummingbird migrates south to Central America, a flight of some 3,500 miles, with 620 of it nonstop across the Gulf of Mexico. To make this part of the journey, it has to eat enough to double its body weight.

Not bad for such a little guy! No wonder the hummingbird is often associated with the achievement of the impossible.

Significance

Key Words: Joy, celebration, love, rapid success, long journeys

The Big Picture: When Hummingbird flies into your life, expect an event that will have you celebrating—a romance, a long trip, or a joyful event or situation. An experience with Hummingbird can signal that you are about to embark on an inner quest or spiritual adventure that ultimately will teach you that you are capable of achieving whatever you set out to do, even if others tell you it's impossible.

Romance: A new romance is on the way. It may not be a relationship with your soul mate, but it definitely will be fun, playful, and will bring you enormous joy. If you're already involved, then Hummingbird's appearance in your life may be telling you to lighten up, to inject more playfulness into your partnership, to rediscover joy.

Finances: Do what you love and the money will follow: Isn't that how the adage goes? Well, it fits the financial arena when Hummingbird darts into your life. If you've been flitting about from one job to another, hoping to find the ideal way to earn a living, then it's time to hover for awhile, to take stock and decide what you really want to do. There's no time like right now to reach for your dream.

Work/Career: This category is closely linked with the one above where Hummingbird is concerned. Read the financial description again, then think about this. Each of us is allotted so many years on the planet. Why work at something you may not be crazy about? What fear is holding you back? Don't listen to the naysayers, the critics. Listen to your own heart. Do whatever makes you joyful.

Health: Your general health is good. But you should pay closer attention to your thoughts and to what you say and take note if you sound bitter or defeated. If you do, then you may want to add zest and joy to your life—and to your thoughts. Any time you find yourself in a negative groove, get out of it by repeating a positive affirmation. Since a hummingbird's diet consists primarily of nectar, you may want to get your sugar checked, too. Diet plays an important role in your health at this time. Is your metabolism too fast? Do you have trouble gaining weight? Have your thyroid checked.

Family: It's time to pay more attention to your kids. They may be at an age when they need your counsel, advice, or just your perspective on their daily lives. You and your kids could be taking a long trip together, perhaps an overseas destination that everyone has wanted to visit.

Creativity: Look to the past for inspiration, but allow yourself to move forward in your daily life. Your intuition plays an important role in your creative voice now. Follow your own heart, your own vision.

Spirituality: Joy is your path toward deeper spirituality.

LADYBUG

Myths, Folklore, Legends

For such a tiny creature, the ladybug boasts an abundance of folklore, perhaps because she's so much cuter than other bugs.

Back in the Middle Ages, farmers considered the ladybug to be a harbinger of good luck for the harvest because she consumed many of the insects that infested their crops.

One popular legend about ladybugs concerns a village eons past whose fields were being threatened by hordes of insects. The villagers prayed for help and, in the eleventh hour, swarms of ladybugs arrived and saved their fields from destruction.

It's said that finding a ladybug is good luck and that it's *really* lucky if a ladybug lands on you. Killing a ladybug, of course, brings bad luck and sickness. The number of spots on a ladybug indicates the number of lucky and happy months that you have ahead of you. If a woman is recently married and a ladybug lands on her hand, then the dots on the bug's back indicates the number of children she'll have.

There's a rhyme about the ladybug that suggests its connection to love and romance: "Fly away east, fly away west, show me where lives the one I love best." The direction in which the ladybug flies is where your true love—or future love—lives.

Facts and Trivia

Ladybugs are actually a type of beetle. They're the most commonly known of all beneficial insects because, as their lore suggests, they eat insects that destroy crops and other vegetation. They go through a complete metamorphosis, so they could fit under the category of transformation, too.

The length of their life cycle depends on external factors—temperature, humidity, food sources—but usually takes three or four weeks or up to six weeks in cooler months. Typically, the female ladybug lays from fifty to three hundred eggs that are light yellow and deposited in clusters of ten to fifty, in aphid colonies. That way, when the eggs hatch in three to five days, the larvae feed on the aphids or on other insects for two or three weeks, then pupate. Adults emerge seven to ten days later. There can be as many as five or six generations in a single year. The adults hibernate in the autumn.

In addition to aphids, ladybugs also feed on mealybugs, spider mites, and eggs of other beetles. A single larva will eat four hundred aphids before it reaches the pupal stage. An adult eats nearly as many before it lays eggs. These numbers add up: Over the course of a ladybug's lifetime, it can eat as many as five thousand aphids.

Ladybugs have an interesting protection from predators: They emit a chemical that other bugs find distasteful. Thanks to this and their particular diet, ladybugs are a natural way to control pests in your garden and yard.

These little creatures could also fit into other categories: camouflage, protection, and transformation.

Significance

Key Words: Luck, harvest, good fortune, transformation

The Big Picture: When Ladybug appears in your life, the meaning depends on the experience itself. Did the ladybug come into your home? Did it settle on your clothing? Your hand? What were you thinking about when this happened? There's a timing element with Ladybug—three to five days or three to six weeks.

Romance: A new romance is likely within the next three to five days or three to six weeks. Even if it's short-lived, it will be joyful and beneficial for you.

Finances: Your income should be increasing shortly. A raise or promotion or both is possible. You could receive an unexpected check or the repayment of a loan. If you've been thinking about refinancing, now is the time to do it.

Work/Career: You're in the right place at the right time. Serendipitous events nudge you in a new, more beneficial direction. Within six weeks, you could be changing jobs or find yourself in a much improved work situation.

Health: The prognosis is excellent. If you have nagging health problems, Ladybug's message is that you're on the mend. If you've been chronically ill, a spontaneous remission is possible at this time .

Family: Get outdoors with your family and loved ones and have fun. Get your kids involved in sports, go hiking and biking, go camping. The point is to do as much as you can with your family that's related to outdoor activities and to the unadulterated pursuit of pleasure and joy.

Creativity: If you've been working steadily on a creative project, then within six weeks you should be done. Your creative adrenaline is at an all-time high right now, so make good use of it!

Spirituality: Your spiritual path involves the joy of discovery. Simple, right?

Brainstorming

These three creatures are such a delight to watch and to be around and are usually so numerous that you won't lack for opportunities to observe and research them firsthand. You can create environments that will attract them, take a drive through the country to observe and photograph them, or take nature walks to get up close and personal.

Before you embark on your personal exploration, create an invocation that you can say or think as you're seeking them out. It may be something as simple as shutting your eyes and imagining the creature coming toward you or it may be a poem or prayer you've written for that animal. Experiment to see what type of invocation works best.

Here are some other suggestions:

Movies, books, plays.

Years ago, Burt Lancaster starred in a strange and wonderful movie called *The Birdman of Alcatraz*. We won't reveal too much about the movie except to say that after you see it, you will always associate birds with freedom and joy.

If you have kids or you're a teacher, engage in playful activities that deal with these three creatures. Draw pictures. Make collages. Head out into the fields for your very own "field trip."

Right attitude.

This is a frame of mind, an instinct, a feeling. It means that when you embark on your exploratory journeys, you should do so with joy and excitement in your heart. Instead of assuming you'll have another encounter, ask instead what *you* can do for the animal.

Honoring Your Animal

With the advent of digital cameras and videocameras, it's possible to make your own photo montages and film clips about animals. You might want to try this and then create a website on the animal you're honoring.

Just poke around on the Internet some time and take a look at some of the wonderful sites on animals. Many of them seem to be created by people whose excitement and passion for the animals they're honoring comes through loud and clear. Sites like these help educate the rest of us. The more educated people are about animals, the faster old beliefs about them will be broken.

9

Intuition, Dreams, Shamanism

EEL, BAT

Shamanism is probably one of the oldest traditions that recognizes and honors the connections between animals and man. To this day, indigenous people around the world practice intricate rituals related to the power of certain animals to do certain things or to bring about certain events and conditions.

Today, numerous workshops and seminars are conducted throughout the Western world that teach these ancient traditions and instruct Westerners how to find their personal power animal or totem and how to interpret their experiences with animals in light of shamanistic traditions. Intuition and the art of dreaming are often vital parts of these ancient traditions, and the appearance of certain animals is a signal that we must pay closer attention to our intuition and the power of our dreams.

Water is the element most closely allied with inner states of consciousness, so animals that live in water are often associated with intuition and dreaming. This would include many kinds of fish, water birds, or mammals that live part of their lives in and around water. It would also include mythological creatures like mermaids or mermen.

On the island of Chiloe in southern Chile, the local fishermen have long believed in mermaids. If the fish are abundant on a given day, then they will see a mermaid facing shore. If the fish are sparse, the mermaid will be facing out to sea. Do the fishermen actually see these mermaids? Well, who knows? The point is that the myth is so strong, so pervasive, that the connection between it and the fishermen is psychic, intuitive, and exists in an inner realm that is inexplicable in ordinary terms.

Our connections with certain types of animals exist in that same realm. How often have you seen a mole? A beaver? An eel? An ibis? To some extent, that depends on where you live or which zoos you frequent (or if you watch *Animal Planet!*). Even if you never see these creatures anywhere but on TV, it's possible to dream about one of them. Each one is connected to intuition, the art of dreaming, the psychic realm, shamanism.

We debated about which animals to include in this chapter for detailed descriptions. At one point, we figured the bat and the deer. At another point, we decided on the eel and the mole. Millie felt we should describe the ibis, which was considered sacred to the Egyptians. In the end, we chose the bat and the eel, two very different creatures that live in two vastly different environments. But both are connected to that strange inner world that we all inhabit when our consciousness detaches from the outer world and enters the realm of the shaman.

EEL

Myths, Folklore, Legends

The legends, myths, and superstitions surrounding the eel are both strange and scarce. That is somehow fitting for a creature about which precious little is really known.

Let's start with the superstitions. In ancient times (of course), the treatments for warts were bizarre and quite varied. But one treatment involved catching an eel, cutting off its head, and squeezing its blood onto the wart. The head of the eel was then supposed to be buried and, as the head rotted within the earth and dissolved, the wart would also disappear.

In Samoa, a popular tale is about a young girl named Sina and an eel and how their relationship resulted in the coconut tree. As tales goes, this one is definitely weird. One day, Sina's mother drew water from a well and an eel was clinging to the side. She took it home to her daughter, who kept it in a bowl, as a pet. When the eel was fully grown and too large for the bowl, it announced that it loved Sina, who was, of course, repulsed by the eel's affections and fled. The eel, a persistent lover, ran after Sina and broke through the various obstacles that her parents placed in its path.

But then Sina reached a village and begged the local chiefs for help, and they killed the eel. As it lay dying, it begged Sina to plant its body near a stone wall. It promised that a tree would grow there and bear fruit and leaves. She was to weave the leaves into fans and mats, a reminder that it would return.

After the villagers ate the eel, she saved its head and planted it in front of her home. Eventually, a tree started growing there and the eel's prophecy was fulfilled: The tree became known as a coconut tree and its leaves are now used to make mats and fans. The coconut allegedly bears the image of an eel: The two hard eyes are the eyes of the eel and the soft eye that's pierced for drinking from the coconut is the eel's mouth.

In the South Pacific, the eel and the flounder are believed to be the first creators of the islands of Tuvalu. This belief is so strong there that eels are taboo for eating.

Among certain tribes in the Philippines, eels are believed to be the souls of the dead. In Europe, it's believed that rubbing your skin with eel oil will allow you to see fairies.

The real mystery of the eel, though, seems to lie in where it spawns.

Facts and Trivia

The Sargasso Sea is a strange, mysterious place. It isn't a sea in the normal sense—that is, it has no definite location, no specific longitude or latitude. Instead, it moves, it drifts, and its location is determined by the changing ocean currents.

In fact, when Columbus reached these deep blue waters of the central North Atlantic, he thought he was close to shore because there was an abundance of floating algae. The algae, a weed, was called *sargassum,* and actually lies hundreds of miles from the North American coast. It covers about two million square miles of ocean and yet, has no fixed location. It happens to be in the same vicinity as the Bermuda triangle, that mysterious area in the Atlantic where ships and planes have vanished mysteriously since the early 1940s.

The sea itself is known as the floating desert. About a third of the Atlantic's plankton is produced here, and although it doesn't have the nutrients to sustain commercially valuable fish, crabs, shrimp, and octopuses live here. It's also the grand bazaar for eels. Where fish like salmon and striped bass migrate from the sea to freshwater rivers to spawn, the eels do it the other way around. Every autumn, large female eels begin a journey that can last for hundreds of miles, down rivers and streams to join male eels and to spawn in the Sargasso.

Females can lay up to 500 million eggs, but because so little is known about eels, there's no estimate about the survival rate of these eggs. When the eggs hatch, the larvae begin a journey toward shore that is almost epic.

During their travels, they develop into glass eels—transparent creatures about an inch long. They then migrate toward the coastal shores to feed and grow.

In Asian countries, the glass eels are considered to be a delicacy, and during the 1990s, a huge industry grew up around them. Eels won't reproduce in captivity, so they have to be netted from the wild. With market prices soaring higher than $300 a pound, anyone with a net headed out to reap quick money. In 1998, the state of New Jersey, which has a large eel population along its coast, banned eel fishing and other coastal states quickly imposed size limits and restricted the eel-fishing season.

Significance

Key Words: Mysterious, intuitive, unusual sexuality, "electric" experiences, hidden, unknown

The Big Picture: If you dream of Eel, you may be entering a period of unusual sexual activity. What is hidden from you may be revealed through synchronicities, dreams, or sexual encounters with a partner with whom you share deep psychic or past-life connections. Listen to y our intuition and attempt to use your dreams to glean information that you need.

Romance: Your sex life heats up! You feel a profound physical attraction to someone and don't hesitate to act on it. You may come together with this person for a specific reason (other than sex), but will need intuitive or dream guidance to figure out what that reason is. You may be as "slippery as an eel" in pinning down what you feel about a partner or a relationship. This relationship will have an "electric" quality to it, as though you experience some sort of psychic or intuitive shock.

Finances: You may be earning more, but it's going out just as fast as you earn it. It's time to figure out your financial priorities, put yourself on a budget, and stick to it. Because of Eel's connection to sex, sexuality, and eroticism, it's possible that your sexual experiences at this time stimulate you to seek new ways to earn money.

Work/Career: Your career seems to follow patterns that are unfamiliar to you. There may be upheavals and sudden disruptions, but these events actually prove quite positive in that they steer you onto a new course that is better suited to your goals. Consider taking a workshop or seminar on the development of your intuition, the study of dreams, or on shamanism.

Health: Consider alternative treatments for a nagging health problem. Acupuncture or yoga may be helpful. It may be time to add more fish to your diet and if you don't like fish, then try Omega-3 supplements. Is the salt content in your diet too high? Get your cholesterol checked.

Family: You feel the need for privacy at this time. Some cocooning at home may be in order or you and your family may want to head out to some remote spot to spend time with each other.

Creativity: Don't hesitate to find and express your unique creative voice. It doesn't matter if you're not doing what everyone else is doing. It's time to pioneer, to trail blaze.

Spirituality: Delve into shamanism. Learn how to lucid dream. Start studying the esoteric—astrology, tarot, the *I Ching*. Your quest has begun.

BAT

Myths, Folklore, Legends

Leave it to Hollywood to take advantage of the terrible superstitions about bats. In the movie *Bats*, the winged creatures living in caves near a Texas town are infected by several brethren that have been genetically altered by—who else?—a mad scientist. Now the bats are smart killers, monstrous in their frenzied sprees. Even though a biologist attempts to save the uninfected bats and talks about what gentle creatures they are, she eventually is out there with her weapons, just like the other humans.

Perhaps because bats are so odd-looking, they have been much maligned in folklore and legend: bats as symbolic of the devil and consorts of witches, as blood-sucking vampires, as a creature that will swallow the sun at the end of the world.

But bats have also been viewed in a more positive light. In China, the bat is considered to be a symbol of good luck and happiness. In fact, the Chinese god of happiness—Fu-xing—is represented by the bat and when he's in human form, five bats are embroidered on his robe. The five bats supposedly symbolize the five blessings of health, wealth, long life, virtue, and a good death.

The Maya thought of the bat as a creature of the underworld and of death. In the book of the Mayas, the *Popol Vuh*, there is reference to a house of bats, the region that a soul must cross to reach the land of the dead. This belief is similar to the one held in shamanistic traditions, where the bat is associated with death—but also with rebirth.

In Medieval Europe, bats were often nailed to doors to ward off demons, witches, and black magic. They were used to treat snakebites and as aphrodisiacs. As nocturnal creatures, they are associated with the hidden, the occult, the psychic and intuitive.

In an Oklahoma Cherokee Indian Legend, animals challenged birds to a ball game. Bear was the captain (of course!). He was also a showoff, who tossed large logs into the air just to show everyone how strong he was. Deer zipped alongside Bear to show (naturally) how fast he could go.

On the bird team, Eagle was the captain. Hawk and Falcon, both of them quite swift in their own right, joined the bird team. The birds were outwardly confident, but secretly were afraid the animals would win.

The birds hovered high in the sky, waiting for the game to begin, when they spotted two furry things, not much larger than mice, scurrying along a tree branch below them. The furry things wanted to play and begged to be allowed on one of the teams. The birds told the furry things that they belonged on the animal team because they had four feet and fur. But the animals didn't want the furry things; they said they weren't fast or strong enough.

The birds didn't want the furry things, either, because they didn't have wings, and of course you had to have wings to be on the bird team. But the birds felt a little sorry for the furry things and took spare leather from a drum head and cut two wing shapes from it. They stretched the leather straps with cane strips and fastened them to the forelegs of the furry things. In case you haven't guessed yet, these furry things were bats, and this is how they came to have wings!

And oh, by the way, Bat caught the ball and carried it to the goal.

Facts and Trivia

These strange but gentle creatures are found on every continent except the Antarctic and are the only mammal capable of true flight. Of the 977 species of bats, only three feed on blood, and they are found in Mexico, Central, and South America. They generally don't bite people and when they do it is painless. They drink about a spoonful of blood. But it's the vampire bats who have given all the rest of them a bad name. Vampire bats are the only ones to hop along the ground, and they can actually run with great dexterity, using their thumbs, wrists, elbows, and feet.

A bat's wings are intriguing. They are like a modified hand, with digits that are elongated to facilitate flight. The thumb is mostly separate from the membrane that connects the other digits. In some species of bats, the membrane joins the legs and the tail and although muscular and tough, it's extremely flexible. A bat's ears are usually quite long. The Microchiroptera bat has ears that are perfectly designed to pick up the sounds produced in echolocation.

Only the Microchiroptera bat uses high frequency echolocation for navigation, hunting, and catching prey. The sounds are made by the larynx and emitted through the mouth or nose leaf. The ears receive the echoes and the brain translates them into information about the location of prey and about its surroundings. The ultrasonic pulses emitted by bats can be quite loud and intense by human standards and vary according to what the bat is doing—hunting, flying, or navigating.

Contrary to the adage, *Blind as a bat,* bats aren't blind. They see well, but their echolocation abilities are more exact than their eyesight. The fruit bat has excellent eyesight.

Many bat species are able to regulate their body temperature so that it falls when they're roosting during the day or during the winter, when food is scarce. Hibernation isn't necessarily continuous, though, as it is with the bear or other mammals.

Several species of bats are solitary loners, others live in small groups, and many others form colonies in caves that number into the thousands. Some even form breeding groups or harems that last throughout the year.

The gestation period in bats runs from forty to sixty days in the smaller species and can be as long as eight months in others. Usually, just one off-spring is produced, but twins occur regularly in some species of bats. The females of many tropical species of bats often congregate in nursing colonies to bear and raise their young.

Bat species make up twenty-five percent of all the species of mammals on earth.

Significance

Key Words: Esoteric, astral, dreams, intuition, rebirth, past-life connections

The Big Picture: When Bat flies into your life, it may be time to step back, detach, and turn inward for awhile. Since the roosting bat, in its upside down position, has a correlation to The Hanged Man in the tarot, it's necessary to look at a relationship or situation from a different perspective or with a completely different attitude. Bat may also be telling you to seek the support of a group of like-minded individuals. You may be entering a period of your life when the night holds great clarity, creativity, and power for you. Listen closely to what you "hear" on an intuitive level. For timing, look at a span of forty to sixty days.

Romance: You meet a special someone in a group to which you belong or at a large meeting or seminar that you attend. This relationship will bring about positive change in your life, but first you may have to confront fears that you have about intimacy.

Finances: You may be moonlighting for awhile. It won't be something you do to make ends meet, but to buy something special for yourself or someone else or to take a trip that you otherwise can't afford. It's also possible that you work two jobs so that you can put away extra money for a rainy day.

Work/Career: You may be changing jobs or your career. It's possible that your work will involve a hospice or some other facet of death and dying. Equally possible is a career in healing, either a conventional profession or something in alternative health.

Health: It may be necessary to change your diet at this time, perhaps by adding more fruits and grains. You also may need to change your sleep schedule, with greater periods of wakefulness at night, supplemented by short naps during the day. It's beneficial at this time to train yourself in dream recall. Important information will come to you in this way.

Family: If you don't have a family of your own, then it's likely you'll become involved with a group of people who are like family to you. If you do have a family, then the females may be getting together to celebrate the birth of a child, and everyone will pitch in to help the mother.

Creativity: You begin doing some of your creative work at night and find that you love the results. It's especially important now to "listen" to your muse.

While you're at it, rent the movie of the same name, with Sharon Stone playing the part of the muse!

Spirituality: The yin, feminine, receptive path is the one to follow at this time. Intuition, imagination, and your psychic connections to everyone and everything around you are heightened. The study of paganism, Wicca, and shamanism will benefit you.

Brainstorming

Eel and Bat hold such esoteric and mystical significance that when you have an experience with one of them, it's time to take decisive steps in your life to deepen that connection. Here are some suggestions on how to do that:

Attend a workshop.

Not just any ol' workshop, but one on shamanism, intuitive development, working with dreams, reincarnation, life after death. The Omega Institute, headquartered in Rhinebeck, New York, or the Institute of Noetic Sciences, started by astronaut Edgar Mitchell, offer various kinds of workshops and seminars around the country on any of these topics.

Movies, books.

There are numerous books on all these topics available at your local bookstore. Suggestions? Start with books by Carlos Castaneda, Hank Friedman, Michael Horner, Patricia Garfield, Carol Bowman, Joseph McMoneagle, John Edwards, Louise Hay, Edgar Cayce, Carolyn Myss, Mona Lisa Schultz. These books will lead you to others.

Movies? You're in for a treat: *Dead Again, The Reincarnation of Peter Proud, Jacob's Ladder, 21 Grams, Sliding Doors.*

Get a psychic reading.

Use word of mouth on this one and avoid 800 lines and Internet psychics. Millie does readings for individuals and her contact information is in the appendix. The town of Cassadaga, Florida, just north of Orlando, is a community of Spiritualists—people who specialize in speaking to the dead. Hazel West Burley does private readings in her home and she's excellent. Both of us have had readings with Hazel. Her contact information is also in the appendix.

Study divination techniques.

Other divination techniques you may want to research include: tarot cards, runes, the *I Ching*, astrology, palmistry, the Medicine Cards. One of our favorite divination techniques is using a dictionary to answer questions. You simply ask your question, focus for a moment, then open a dictionary and point at random to something on the page.

More often than not, you point at a word or phrase that concerns your question.

It takes a little practice, though, and in the beginning you may point at words that don't seem to have anything at all to do with your question. Don't get discouraged. Just set the dictionary aside and try again later. We have found that virtually anything can be used to glean divinatory information, and the system you use isn't as important as the intent that you bring to the process. Be sincere. Ask pertinent questions.

Honoring Your Animal

How do you honor an eel or a bat? Through art, music, education, or keeping a journal. But the most personal way is get out and observe the animals within their environments.

To some extent, observing eels or bats depends on where you live. Some zoos have bat exhibits and marine zoos often have eels. But check your community's resources for more specific information.

10

Spirituality and Healing

DOLPHIN, DEER

Dogs, cat, birds, mice, hamsters, geckos, lizards, any and all animals who are our companions actually belong in this category. In fact, any animal that touches our lives or whose lives we touch are healers and spiritual guides.

In *Kindred Spirits,* author and veterinarian Allen M. Schoen tells a profoundly moving story about a golden retriever, Megan, who was his companion for ten years. She was a stray who had the worst case of heartworms that he'd ever seen. He promised her that if she would help him help her get well, he would adopt her and make her his companion. She got better and she literally became his vet assistant.

"Over the ten years we spent together, Megan administered to a veritable Noah's ark of animals. She became my unofficial nurse and partner. She seemed to feel it was her job to offer tenderness to any wounded or needy animal." She often accompanied Schoen on his night rounds and emergency calls and learned the art of "cautious approach," so that she didn't frighten the patient. She became his guide, Schoen writes, "on a journey to a deeper, clearer perception of all that is truly considered healing."

Many of us who enjoy animal companions probably have had at least one with whom we share a special and deep attachment. Sometimes, the animal enters our lives at a time when we badly need understanding, unconditional love, and a deeper connection with the natural flow of life. Other times, the animal comes to teach us something or to learn from us. Occasionally, if we're really fortunate, we develop a relationship with an animal who doesn't live with us, but whose path crosses ours for some reason.

Trish's family used to live on a lake in South Florida. Dozens of Muscovi ducks lived on and around the lake. Generally, these ducks aren't well-liked in South Florida. Many homeowners consider them to be pests because they leave their droppings everywhere, will eat almost anything, and reduce lawns to nothing. They're quite prolific and often make nests in yards, atriums, under bushes, right in the homeowner's yard. They lay at least a dozen eggs and after about six weeks, the eggs hatch one after another. The mother spends about a day in the nest with her new chicks, then heads out into the world, the little ducklings hurrying after her.

The ducklings are often fragile and the last one to emerge usually gets left behind because the mother already has abandoned the nest. In one nest, a runt got left behind before it had fully emerged from its egg. Trish and her daughter, Megan, brought the chick indoors shortly after it hatched, put the chick in a box with its eggshell, and turned on a lamp to keep it warm. They called the chick Amy.

Amy, a soft, furry yellow, flourished in the box. She ate the inside of her eggshell on the first day of her life and by the second day, was ready to join her flock. But the mother rejected her, so Trish and Megan brought her back into the atrium and began to raise her with seed and grain. Within a few weeks, there were other injured chicks from another flock in the atrium clinic, and Amy found a family that raised her. Within a few months, she began taking care of younger, injured ducklings and when they were ready to leave the nest, she took them out into the world. Over a period of months, Amy returned to the atrium and mothered four or five different sets of chicks.

She eventually migrated down to the other end of the lake and took up residence in the yard of another duck lover, a woman who owned a goose.

The goose and Amy shared the same maternal instincts and were often seen waddling together through the neighborhood, with ducklings trailing behind them. Since it's difficult to tell the gender of Muskovis until they're fully grown, it finally became apparent that Amy was actually Amos!

Amos taught Trish and Megan that love and altruism exists between animals as surely as it does among humans.

Altruistic acts among wild animals are a hotly debated issue. But, as authors Jeffrey Moussaieff Masson and Susan McCarthy note in their marvelous book, *When Elephants Weep,* these acts do happen. Old lionesses who can no longer hunt for themselves are sometimes sustained for years because younger lions share their kills with them. Altruistic acts have been observed among red foxes, mongooses, gorillas, elephants, chimps, and among whales and dolphins. The latter is also known for its altruistic acts toward humans.

When young Elian Gonzalez fled Cuba on a rickety boat with his mother and headed for the U.S. ninety miles away, the boat sank and Elian clung to a piece of the boat while everyone else drowned. He was helped by a pod of dolphins that kept the piece of wood afloat until he was rescued, a fact that undoubtedly contributed to the boy's mystique.

And altruism is one of the reasons we chose Dolphin for this chapter. This incredible mammal could just as easily go into the chapter on joy or on intuition or on creativity and self-expression. But at the heart of it, the dolphin is about spirituality and healing.

DOLPHIN

Myths, Folklore, Legends

The abundant mythology and folklore surrounding dolphins dates back at least to the ancient Greeks, who believed that dolphins were gods and goddesses. One legend is that a group of men planned to abduct and sell Dionysus into slavery and when he uncovered the plot, he called on a divine power to intervene. The potential abductors dived into the sea, were turned into dolphins, and ever since have been incapable of doing harm.

Another myth explains the origin of the constellation Delphinus. When Poseidon (Neptune) wanted to marry Amphitrite, she refused and fled to Mount Atlas. He sent out people to find her, and it was Delphinus who accomplished the task and brought her back to him. He eventually married her and expressed his gratitude to Delphinus by declaring the dolphin to be sacred and placing its image among the stars. The constellation is composed of nine stars, which are believed to correspond to the nine muses, which explains the dolphin's connection to creativity.

Arion, a Greek poet and musician, was on his way to Corinth when the boat crew decided to murder him and take his money. He begged them to take the money and spare his life, but they refused and offered him one last wish. He asked to sing before dying and as soon as his song was finished, he hurled himself into the sea. A dolphin heard his music and rescued him, carrying him to shore on its back.

Among indigenous people in the Peruvian Amazon, the magnificent pink river dolphin is believed to be able to assume human form on the night of the full moon. It comes ashore as a man dressed in white clothing, with a white hat to cover its blowhole, and seduces the most beautiful woman in the village. This legend is thought to have evolved to explain pregnancy out of wedlock. *The dolphin did it!*

Facts and Trivia

Dolphins are mammals with big smiles: That's how one child described them. Like whales, they're found in every ocean and even in some rivers and lakes. The Amazon *boto,* a fresh water dolphin as pink as bubble gum, inhabits the rivers of South America. The nearly blind Ganges *susu* is a fresh water dolphin that inhabits the Ganges River.

All dolphins have a beak-like snout with conical teeth, and are usually about six feet in length. The males are several inches longer. The largest dolphin is the bottlenose, which can reach more than nine feet and nearly five hundred pounds.

Their bodies are sleek, smooth, hairless, and slightly rubbery to the touch. They feed on fish—mackerel, sardines, squid—and have a distinct preference for herring, which is used in many dolphin centers as treats. Dolphins usually surface every few minutes to breathe air through the blowhole on top of their heads. The exhalation is a strange, explosive sound, startling the first time you hear it. They can hold their breath for long periods of time and are capable of rapid, deep dives of more than a thousand feet.

Mating among dolphins usually occurs in the spring. The gestation period runs from eleven to twelve months, with the calf delivered tail-first. Quite often, there are nurse dolphins who aid in the delivery of the calf and help it surface to take its first breaths.

Communication and vocalization among dolphins captivated the interest of neurologist and researcher John Lily in the fifties and sixties. He established a dolphin research center in the Virgin Islands and attempted to communicate with dolphins in their own language. His research led him on an unexpected spiritual path that caused other scientists to dismiss his work. But among many people, Lily remains the father of dolphin research even though he is no longer in the dolphin research business. He was quoted as saying that he "didn't want to run a concentration camp for highly developed beings."

Dolphins have a specialized mechanism in their nasal passages, just below the blow hole, that enables them to emit short, pulse-type noises called clicks. The clicks can be produced in rapid succession and are used as a form of sonar or echolocation, similar to that of bats. The U.S. military, forever opportunistic, has used dolphins to locate deep water mines. Dolphins also make high-pitched whistles to communicate emotional states.

There's a lot of controversy about whether dolphins are as intelligent as man. The fact is that they display the very qualities that define human intelligence. They're able to make decisions on the basis of information, just as we do. They demonstrate the ability to invent, plan ahead, to be creative, abilities man also has. They have a highly complex social structure, just as we do. Their capacity for sheer joy probably surpasses ours and their altruism undoubtedly surpasses man's as well. If that isn't intelligence, then what is??

In recent years, a spate of research has shown the benefits of Animal Assisted Therapy, where animals become companions to people who are ill, handicapped, and recovering from illness. This area of study has expanded to the elderly, handicapped and terminally ill children, and to people suffering from everything from AIDS to cancer and Alzheimer's. Not surprisingly, dolphins have been shown to be excellent in Animal Assisted Therapy with children who have various educational, emotional, and physical needs.

Dolphins Plus in Key Largo, Florida is known worldwide for its dolphin swim program. It offers both structured swims—guaranteed interaction with the dolphins—and unstructured swims, where the dolphins decide whether they want anything to do with you! The other facet of Dolphins Plus is a program for special needs kids, which is now called Island Dolphin Care (www.islanddolphincare.org).

The program was created by Deena Hoagland, whose son, Joe, had had a stroke after his third open heart surgery and wasn't responding well to traditional therapy. She and her husband Peter brought three-year-old Joe to Dolphins Plus in the hope that being with dolphins might motivate him to use the weakened left side of his body. Joe eventually was able to have a normal life and Deena decided that dolphins might be able to help others as well.

Quoting from the Island Dolphin Care website: "The dolphins are catalysts that provide unconditional love and support. The program also provides unique educational experiences that often allow children to become more expressive and to develop closer bonds with parents, doctors, and therapists upon returning home."

Even for children without special needs and for adults of any age, swimming with dolphins is a unique and spiritually enriching experience. Millie and Trish's family have all participated in the dolphin program in Key Largo, and Trish and her daughter also swam with dolphins on the island of Margarita, off the coast of Venezuela. There is something inexplicably magnificent about immersing yourself in a dolphin's world, surrounded by their clicks and soft explosions of air, and being nudged into a playfulness that makes you feel like you're five years old.

If you swim with dolphins in a setting like Dolphins Plus, you may feel conflicted, as we did, about dolphins being used in this way. During our dolphin swim, we discussed this with one of the trainers. She told us that the dolphins at the center had been rescued—they were injured or sick—and that the dolphins had chosen to stay. At one time, the center was open to the canal that feeds into the ocean, but due to boat traffic, the center has erected a fence to keep the dolphins in. We were told that when a hurricane threatens the Keys, the dolphins are released into the ocean, where they are safer.

Significance

Key Words: Joy, spiritual awakening, playfulness, altruism, sexuality

The Big Picture: When Dolphin swims into your life, then it's time to add plenty of joy and playfulness into whatever you do. It may signal the beginning of a sexual relationship that is fun and playful above all else. It also could indicate that you should start volunteering for a charity, animal shelter, or some other service-oriented organization. You're entering a more creative period of your life and now have the ability to realize your deepest desires.

Romance: Lucky you! You're in for a real treat when your dolphin experience relates to romance. Okay, this may not be a soul mate relationship (although it could be), but it definitely qualifies as important. Through this new partner, you learn to lighten up on yourself and others, to seek joy and creative fulfillment, and begin to realize how important spiritual and psychic connections are with partners. Your sexuality soars and you learn a deeper appreciation for sensuality in all facets of your life.

Finances: New creative opportunities open up related to the creative arts, such as music and writing. You begin to understand that money is only energy and that you can manifest it very easily when you're doing what you love. Play and joy are important facets of your new financial journey.

Work/Career: Bottom line? You're working too hard and have misplaced or lost your sense of joy in your daily work. It's time to delve into the waters of your own unconscious to find the answers and information you need at this time. Dream recall and interpreting your dreams are important now.

Health: If you already have an exercise routine, then you may need to approach it more playfully, instead of as a drudgery. If you don't have an exercise routine, then get started today. It doesn't have to be anything complicated; go with your intuition. If you enjoy swimming, then swim. If you like walking, then walk. Do what comes naturally, but do it regularly. Be attentive to your thoughts, beliefs, and emotions. All of these things have a direct bearing on your health. Do not settle for a first opinion. Seek second opinions. Look for alternative health options.

Family: Friends, relatives, even neighbors may be part of your extended family. If you're a woman who has been trying to get pregnant, then Dolphin's appearance is an excellent portent and hints at a deeply spiritual link between you and your future child.

Creativity: Music, communication, and animals may play vital roles in your creative endeavors now. You benefit through water sports or living near water. The flow of your emotions is crucial to your creative voice.

Spirituality: You're called upon to share your spiritual resources with others. Part of your spiritual path may involve working with environmental causes.

DEER

Myths, Folklore, Legends

The spirituality and healing that Deer symbolizes have a different texture than that of Dolphin. This creature embodies spirituality and healing in terms of magic, innocence, wisdom, and immortality, and has a rich mythological tradition.

Among the ancient Japanese, deer were considered to be messengers of the gods. So it's only fitting that in Nara, the ancient capital of Japan (between A.D. 710-784) there is a park set aside called Deer Park, where more than a thousand deer roam freely, mingling with people. Buddha first preached in the deer park at Sarnath and close to the Nara deer park stands the world's largest bronze statue of Buddha, in the Todaiji Temple.

Among the Pawnee tribe, the deer is thought to be a guide to the light of the sun, the giver of life. This belief was echoed in ancient Mexico, where deer were often depicted carrying the sun. An indigenous tribe in Columbia believe that after death, the human soul travels into a deer.

The deer was sacred to Aphrodite, Artemis, Athene, Diana, and to Apollo. In the Aztec world, the god of hunting was accompanied by a two-headed deer. In shamanism, the deer symbolizes gentleness, beauty, sensitivity, and acute observation. You get the general idea. These creatures are special precisely because they seem to embody the gentleness that we, as a species, may have misplaced or, worse, lost altogether.

Facts and Trivia

To reach Key West, Florida, you have to cross an island called Big Pine Key. What distinguishes Big Pine from the other keys is that it's a Key deer refuge and every few miles, there are signs posted reminding drivers that they are in a refuge for the Key deer and that to date, so many deer have been killed by cars. It's a shocking sight to see these numbers.

The Key deer is the smallest deer in North America, weighing in at just three or four pounds when born. Although Big Pine has the most Key deer, they're also found on No Name Key and some of the lower Florida keys. There are perhaps 800 Key deer left, which makes them an endangered species. There's more about them in Chapter Fourteen ("Endangered Animals").

The white-tailed deer is the antithesis of the Key deer in terms of population. It's the most common deer in the U.S. and is found throughout North America from southern Canada through Central America and as far south as Bolivia. It has good eyesight and hearing, but its sense of smell is extremely well developed, with numerous scent glands on its legs. These deer have been known to run at speeds up to forty miles an hour, are strong swimmers, and are edgy and shy.

When we Googled the phrase, white-tailed deer, it was distressing to see how many hunting sites came up. Granted, white-tailed deer are pests in many states and one of the most efficient—and lucrative ways—to control overpopulation is by harvesting through hunting. On one website, however, the validation for hunting deer smacks of human egocentrism: "Annual harvest exceeds 300,000 in several states and in Nebraska has been about 28,000 since 1987. A more important measure is the amount of recreation provided. ... The monetary impact is also substantial. Deer hunters spent about $1.5 million for permits alone in 1990, and about $1.2 million of this was attributable to whitetails. The total amount spent on whitetail hunting and associated activities in Nebraska is probably near $7 to $8 million annually." The site then goes on to detail what a hunter should be aware of when hunting for white-tailed deer.

If you believe in the idea that animals are on the planet for human recreation, it comes back to what we consider the old paradigm about animals: "If you care to believe many of the ethnologists, animal behaviorists, and other members of the scientific world, animals are basically nonthinking, nonfeeling, nonexpressive creatures," writes veterinarian Allen M. Schoen in his book *Kindred Spirits*. And this kind of thinking, Schoen points out, dates back to Plato and Aristotle.

Aristotle defined a hierarchy that is reprehensible. Male humans were at the top of the food chain, just below divinity, followed by female humans, slaves, and children. The existence of animals was "predicated on the service of humans," writes Schoen.

As Jane Goodall and Marc Bekoff point out in their book, *The Ten Trusts,* all of us raised in the Judeo-Christian belief system "have taken it for granted that Earth and all its riches, including animals, were created for our benefit." Until this belief is obliterated, particularly in the U.S, we will be an aggressive nation that wages war, invades sovereign countries, and refuses to acknowledge that all life—even that life which Aristotle relegated to the very bottom of the hierarchy—has the right to fulfill its potential.

Significance

Key Words: Gentle spirituality, intuitive, camouflage and protection, consciousness, altered states

The Big Picture: At this time, hostility, anger, and placing blame on others has no place in your life. If you feel any of these emotions, acknowledge them, feel whatever you feel, then get to the root of what has caused them. It may be necessary to blend in for awhile, to camouflage yourself within your environment or social group. Observe. Listen. Use all of your senses to understand what's going on. Then make your decision and get on with the business of life.

Romance: Your desire for someone else comes and goes. It fluctuates with the season, the time of day, your mood, your priorities. You're looking for the really deep connections in a relationship; sex just for the sake of sex is okay for awhile, but not what you're looking for as a steady diet. Your spiritual beliefs play into your romantic partnerships.

Finances: It's important to you at this time to be earning money in a way that is in line with your deepest beliefs. Once you do this, your prosperity increases.

Work/Career: Are you being true to yourself? Are you working in a job or career that is in line with your principles? If you're an employer, it may be time to instill more gentleness in your managing techniques.

Health: Have your hearing and your eyesight checked. If you wear glasses or contacts, you may need to have your prescription changed. You should spend more time now preparing your food and eating your meals. Avoid fast food restaurants and eating on the run. A regular exercise routine is called for. Swimming or walking daily would be a good place to start.

Family: If you've been trying to start a family, then Deer's appearance is an excellent harbinger. Timing? The next twenty-eight days look good and so do the months between October and December. At this time, the women in your life play an important role, particularly female relatives. Your relationship with your daughter or daughters, if you have them, need special attention and nurturing now.

Creativity: Yin energy is called for. Dream work is beneficial now. Take a workshop or seminar in dream recall, lucid dreaming, or how to "astral" travel. Explore your inner world. Read. Study. Learn what you can at this time.

Spirituality: It's time to explore and define your spiritual beliefs and to live in accordance with these beliefs.

Brainstorming

If you dream of or have an experience with Dolphin or Deer, it's to your advantage to enhance and deepen your connection with that animal. There are a number of ways to do this.

Our friend Vivian, mentioned in a story about Jackson, the abused dog, makes an annual pilgrimage from Savannah to the Florida Keys to swim with dolphins at Dolphins Plus. She does this for spiritual cleansing and healing. Her home is decorated with dolphin motifs. They're on her walls, her towels, her T-shirts. They are part of her daily meditation. Perhaps because she's so conscious and aware of the role that dolphins have played in her life, she attracts experiences with dolphins. Her home backs up to a salt marsh on one of the barrier islands near Savannah and sometimes during the winter months, dolphins make their way into the marsh and awaken her at night with their joyful splashing and their songs. On her way to work in the morning, when the tide is high, she sometimes sees them. When she does, she knows it's going to be a good day, filled with spiritual insights.

Another friend has an affinity for deer and makes beautiful wood carvings of the animals that decorate his home and that he gives away to friends at Christmas and birthdays. He sometimes treks deep into the woods in the middle of winter and sits quietly and patiently, knowing that if he waits long enough, he will spot a deer.

People who have encounters with dolphins, deer, or any of the other animals associated with spirituality and healing seem to be on a particular path that demands self-knowledge and insight and an awareness of the ways in which humans and animals are connected. It's not unusual for these people to become vegans, animal activists, and peace activists. We find it especially interesting that one of the Democratic candidates for president, Dennis Kucinich, is a vegetarian and the only candidate who has proposed creating a Department of Peace.

If you've had an experience with a dolphin, deer, or any other animal that falls under the category of spirituality and healing, here are some suggestions for deepening that connection:

Get involved.

Speak up, and act on your convictions. Join spiritual groups. Strengthen your connections with people who share your beliefs. The Internet facilitates these kinds of relationships, so use it! Technology allows complete strangers to forge bonds and unite because of their common interests.

Consumer power.

Use it. Boycott companies and products that have practices you find personally offensive. Consumer power brought attention to the number of companies who used animal testing for their products and today, there are far fewer than there were twenty years ago.

John Robbins' seminal book, *Diet for a New America,* brought to light the heinous practices of chicken and cattle slaughterhouses. Although these techniques—like debeaking and the feeding of antibiotics to animals—are still practiced, it's now possible to walk into your local grocery store and find products labeled, *Free roaming chickens, vegetarian eggs.*

But for some of us, even more humane farming isn't acceptable. "Is it ridiculous to care that twenty-four million chickens are killed *every twenty-four hours* in the United States?" asks Jeffrey Moussaieff Masson in *The Pig Who Sang to the Moon.* "That is almost nine billion chickens for the year 2002. As for pigs, there are 268,493 killed every twenty-four hours in the U.S. alone, for a total of 99,236,800 in the year 2002."

Masson, like other animal welfare activists, tackles important issues about animal farming and his stance is utterly clear: Killing animals for food is wrong. "It just makes no sense to me that we would want to care for animals in a compassionate manner, live with them and get to know them as individuals, then turn around and simply kill them for food," he writes.

Consumer spending fuels the Western economy. So use the power that you have. Masson provides information on the "merchants of greed" — corporate giants that control the food industry. Consider boycotting these companies: Tyson Foods (largest poultry producers); IBP, Inc. (largest meatpacking company); ConAgra (second largest food manufacturer); Smithfield Foods (world's largest pork producer); Cargill and Monsanto (they raise cattle, hogs, turkeys, and chickens for the slaughterhouse); Philip Morris (the cigarette manufacturer is also the world largest food manufacturer).

Request higher guidance.

There's a difference between *religion* and *spirituality*. In the first, you follow the dictates of a church; in the second, you follow the whispers of your heart, your soul. In both, however, there is a belief in a higher authority—God, Allah, Christ consciousness, or All That Is. In requesting higher guidance, use whatever techniques work for you, within the context of your spiritual/religious beliefs.

Honoring Your Animal

Here's the dilemma. Once you begin to realize that animals are our teachers—rather than our underlings, our chattel—your experiences take on an entirely different tone. With each experience, with each book that you read, each website that you visit, each story that you hear, you're confronted with a dichotomy.

It goes something like this. Let's say that you've gotten past the quagmire of *food*. You've become a vegan—no meat, no chicken, no turkey, no fish, no eggs or other dairy products. Or perhaps you've come up with some other mixture—fish and dairy products, but nothing else.

Now ask yourself: What about clothing? Go through your closet. Do you own a leather jacket? Leather shoes? A leather purse or wallet? Leather is hide. Where do hides come from? Animals. Are animals killed to supply leather?

Yes. Or take your favorite down comforter. It's filled with goose down. No harm done, right?

"Although most down comes from birds butchered for their meat, some are plucked alive," writes Jeffrey Moussaieff Masson. "The rippers who take these delicate feathers from live birds are none too delicate in their methods. Since they must pluck over one hundred goose a day, you can imagine how careful they are."

What about wool clothing? Even though sheep aren't killed for their wool, they are sheared and it hurts.

You can see how this process of scrutiny may take you into places you may not want to venture. Even though we've strayed a bit from dolphins and deer, it all deserves our attention.

A few years ago, Trish's teenage nephew asked her: "Aunt Trish, do you believe that animals have souls?"

"Of course they have souls."

"But the Bible says that only human beings have souls."

"Well, forget the Bible for a moment." She pointed at his dog. "Can you look at your dog and honestly tell me you don't think she has a soul?"

He looked at his dog—and laughed. "Oh, come on. It's ridiculous to think a dog—or any other animal—has a soul."

Once you open up to the world of animals, you will encounter great resistance from every side, even from within your own family. After all, if we admit that animals have souls, or that they feel emotional pain, then how can we eat them?

In honoring an animal connected to spirituality and healing, you may have to deal with these kinds of issues and questions.

11

Camouflage
and Protection

PORCUPINE, OCTOPUS

O ne of the first things we learn about in elementary school science is that camouflage is nature's way of protecting wildlife. From lizards to turtles, preying mantises to chipmunks, to polar bears, lions, even the octopus, nature has done her part in endowing the species with ways to camouflage and protect themselves.

Take the lizard. From the gecko to the iguana to your basic garden variety lizard, these reptiles blend in. Sometimes, nature's method of camouflage and protection is through mimicry, as with the scarlet king snake. This snake is harmless and is patterned in such a way so that it's often mistaken for the highly venomous coral snake.

Mimicry is one of nature's favorite camouflages. The harmless king snake looks very much like the venomous coral snake. The only difference in their appearance is in the yellow and red rings. If the rings touch, it's a coral snake. The sort of mimicry is prevalent among butterflies, too. The viceroy mimics the monarch butterfly, with just a very small difference between the two: The viceroy has a narrow black band across each hind wing.

The rugged darkling beetle, which is found in California, looks exactly like a piece of rough bark, the perfect camouflage because this beetle lives under oak bark. The "rugged" part of the equation is evident in some of the related family members, which can remain alive in captivity for months without food or water. Precisely because of its strange look, these beetles are common sights in Mexican shops, where they're sold as jewelry.

One of the more distasteful insects, at least from a human point of view, are head lice. In tropical climates, there are occasionally infestations of head lice spread by combs, brushes, and head rests that infect hundreds of elementary school children. The lice are difficult to see in human hair because they're small, cling tightly to the hair strands, and tend to blend into the color of the hair.

Vipers use their camouflage to lie in wait for their prey. They coil beside a mammal trail or in the branches of a tree or beside some desert shrubs and in all cases, their camouflage is so perfect that you don't know they're there until they move.

The walkingstick is extremely well camouflaged. It resembles a stick or a twig and some tropical species look like leaves. The northern mole cricket is a burrower and looks just like the mud and soil where it burrows.

The praying mantis is another perfectly camouflaged animal. Most are green or brown, blending in ideally in their surroundings, but some mimic the colors of bright flowers or other types of colored foliage. The female, of course, is notorious for her habit of biting off the head of the male while they're mating. That certainly ends the possibility of any domestic arguments!

For this chapter, we selected the porcupine and the octopus. The first represents protection and the second represents camouflage.

PORCUPINE

Myths, Folklore, Legends

One of the best known tales about the porcupine concerns how it got its quills. There are many variations of this story among indigenous people and the storyline goes something like this:

Porcupine used to have fur and was quite beautiful. Her beauty made the other animals jealous and she eventually became quite vain, what with all the other animals telling her what a cutie she was. She often stopped by a stream to admire her reflection and the Great Spirit saw this and decided it was time to punish Porcupine. The Great Spirit took away Porcupine's gorgeous fur and covered her body with ugly quills.

Among Australia's Aborigines, the quill story has something of a darker twist to it. In this version, Piggiebillah the Porcupine was once a man. When he got old, he lived among younger villagers, many of whom he had known when they were children. They were strong and tireless, able to hunt and to travel long distances while Piggiebillah stayed at the camp. No one gave Piggiebillah food, yet he remained well-nourished and surprisingly healthy. No one in the village could figure out why.

So several villagers followed him one morning when he left camp and saw him hide behind a large rock. As a young woman came along the path, Piggiebillah jumped out and sank his spear into her. He dragged her away, ate her arms and her legs and hid the rest of her body so that he could feast on the remains later. Finally, the villagers understood why so many people had disappeared from their tribe and why the old man remained so healthy!

A secret meeting was held and on a night when there wasn't a moon, the village men gathered around Piggiebillah as he slept and stabbed him to death with their spears. They broke his arms and his legs and beat him until he lay motionless.

Once the men had left, Piggiebillah dragged himself into the darkness until he came to the burrow of the trapdoor spider. He fell down its hole and remained at the bottom until his wounds were healed. But he couldn't pull the spears out of his body and his broken bones wouldn't mend. When he finally emerged from the hole, no one recognized him. He crawled, his broken legs splayed out, and the spears stuck up from his back. He had to dig for his food with his hands, satisfying his hunger with insects and bits of food. He had turned into Porcupine.

These stories underscore Porcupine's association with humility in shamanistic and pagan traditions.

Facts and Trivia

The porcupine is a rodent and there are three species that have slight physiological differences. All have quills, however, are nocturnal, and live in burrows, crevices, and caves.

The American porcupine is herbivorous, slow-moving, and nonaggressive. Its quills, some thirty thousand of them, lie smoothly against its back, unless it's alarmed or threatened. Then the quills rise. They detach easily and remained embedded because of the small barbs along their length. When the porcupine feels threatened, it buries its snout between its front legs and turns around, so that its rear is facing the enemy. They don't seek out anyone to injure. The quills are only for self-preservation and defense.

The porcupine has two distinct front teeth that are used for gnawing. These teeth grow continuously throughout their lives, which may be why they gnaw on wood—to keep the teeth trimmed down.

These animals are solitary creatures, unless it's the mating season, which happens in the fall and winter. The males issue a mating call, and interested females call back. Part of the courting rituals involves a rubbing of noses as the male and female approach each other.

Porcupines aren't especially prolific—just one or two babies are born after a gestation period of seven months. Only the Mom raises the young. The quills on the babies start hardening within the first hour of life.

These animals are basically gentle loners, who apparently enjoy whatever they're doing, whether it's foraging for barks, plants, fruits, or gnawing on bark and wood. They have a fondness for salt, and if you have wooden paddles in your garage or backyard that have been in salt water, the porcupine will find them and gnaw on them.

Significance

Key Words: Humility, gentleness, curiosity, protection

The Big Picture: You may be coming up against people whose barbed sarcasm hurts or offends you. Or, it's equally possible that you make someone else feel that way. But if the latter is true, it's likely the other person has deeply annoyed you and you're letting them know you don't appreciate it. Porcupine's appearance sometimes means that you need to be more curious about people and things that lay outside your immediate circle. A seven-month timing cycle can be involved when Porcupine appears.

Romance: If you're emerging from a period of solitude, then you're in for a treat! It's likely that you meet someone whose voice you enjoy or who communicates in a way that pleases you. Even if you're hesitant at first about getting involved, mutual chemistry wins you over.

Finances: If someone close is discouraging you about trying something new that could bring in more money—but which also may be a risk—ignore them. You have to evaluate this situation on your own. It would be detrimental to make a decision you don't want to make just to please someone else.

Work/Career: Re-read the finances section above. What is said there also applies here, since work is how you earn your daily bread. You may find that you're better suited for work at night, that your body rhythm is more in tune with the darkness. If you've been considering a job change, then now is the time to nose around and brainstorm about the type of work you really want to do.

Health: It's possible that your metabolism may be too slow or too fast at this time. You may want to get your thyroid checked or try acupuncture to restore the chi balance in your body. Also, watch your salt intake. It's a good idea to notice how your emotions impact your health. If you find yourself being sarcastic toward others, look for the root emotional cause.

Family: Are you or someone around you trying to get pregnant? If so, then you may get your wish within the next seven months or by fall. If you already have kids, then now is the time to get out and have fun with them! Slow down the pace of your life and try to perceive the world the way a child does, with an innocent curiosity.

Creativity: Whether you make your living at a creative pursuit or it's a passion or hobby, you may need more solitude now to find your creative voice. It's a good idea to change your sleep patterns, too, if at all possible. Try working at night for a few hours. You should lighten up on yourself and approach your creativity with a sense of playfulness, curiosity, and exploration.

Spirituality: Right now, your spiritual path lies in solitude and inner work. Meditation would be beneficial and so would any kind of body work like tai chi and yoga. Once you've done the inner work, you'll be ready to move back into the larger world and share what you have discovered.

OCTOPUS

Myths, Folklore, Legends

Jules Verne figured it out in 1870: Octopuses are terrifying to most of us. And in *20,000 Leagues Under the Sea*, Verne's submarine, the *Nautilus*, is attacked by giant octopuses and the crew has to fight them off. Verne did his homework on giant sea creatures, talking about legends of a giant octopus that were common among Nordic fishermen. The giant cephalopod was supposed to be a mile in length, with tentacles that were forty to sixty feet long.

Legends and lore about giant sea monsters were fairly common among seafaring people. The Fijian shark-god, Dakuwanga, supposedly met his match in the giant octopus. After a lengthy battle, the octopus won and Dakuwonga promised never to attack the inhabitants of Kandavu—a Fijian island—again.

In Norwegian folklore, Kraken was a sea monster that was part octopus and part crab. In Hawaiian folklore, Kanaloa is the Hawaiian creator and god of the underworld, a teacher of magic. His shape is that of an octopus. In Pacific mythology, Na Kika is the octopus god of the Gilbert Islands. He supposedly used his many arms to shove earth up from the bottom of the sea to form the islands.

J.K. Rowling, known for her use of mythology and folklore in her Harry Potter books, has a giant squid living in the lake outside of Hogwart's.

In contemporary times, the word octopus is often used to describe someone who is gangly (all arms) or for testosterone-driven macho men who grope women. Interestingly, when Arnold Schwarzenegger entered the gubernatorial race in California and was accused of sexual harassment by a number of women, it came to light that in Hollywood he was known as the "octopus."

Facts and Trivia

These creatures have long terrified human beings. Even if you remove the sea monster factor—their size, which is greatly exaggerated in myth and legend—they're still formidable just because they look, well, so incredibly *strange*. And their skills and talents are just as weird.

Just what *is* an octopus? Sea monster or intelligent sea creature? Leviathan or prankster? The octopus's closest cousin is the squid, but it also shares ancestry with clams, oysters, and snails. It lost its shell way back when and developed, instead, long, dexterous arms lined with as many as two hundred suckers apiece. The arms are the equivalent of the human tongue and the elephant trunk, flexible because of the coordinated contraction and relaxation of numerous muscles. In each of its eight arms, the octopus has four sets of muscles, and each sucker on each of those arms consists of ten thousand neurons.

"It's as though each arm has a separate brain," writes Eugene Linden in *The Octopus and the Orangutan.* "Some scientists think that it is possible to teach one octopus arm a behavior than another arm does not know. There are also stories of octopus arms, detached from the body, that still perform functions such as passing food up suckers."

When confronted with danger, octopuses can alter their skin pigment so they blend into their environment. According to Linden, octopuses can "change their appearance twenty times a minute," an ability that comes from their specialized pigment cells. It's the cephalopod answer to a shape-shifter, the ultimate camouflage system. It can even adjust the texture of its skin from "frilly to smooth depending on what disguise the animal wants to assume."

Linden makes a convincing case for octopus intelligence, relating stories about octopuses that can pick locks, negotiate mazes, recognize their caretakers, and engage in play. But the bottom line is that the octopus is a master of camouflage and nature has endowed it with an impressive bag of tricks to survive in the sea.

The mating habits of the octopus are as strange as everything else about them. The animal's third right arm has a spoon-like tip for depositing sperm inside the mantle of the female in a mating process that takes hours. The female lays anywhere from 20,000 to 100,000 eggs inside her den and tends to them for months, until they finally hatch. She dies shortly afterward. The poor male is believed to die a few months after mating. It's as if this creature's entire life culminates around the mating and the hatching. And then that's it.

Adult octopuses grow to about fifty pounds around Alaska and up to a hundred pounds in the Pacific Northwest. In the 1960s, however, a large octopus was captured off the coast of British Columbia that weighed nearly 160 pounds and had arms that were twenty-three feet long. But so far, the only place where an octopus a mile long has been reported is in the imagination of Jules Verne.

Significance

Key Words: Camouflage, eccentric, original thinker, manual dexterity, sexual peak

The Big Picture: Unless you're a scuba diver who dives to impressive depths or are fortunate enough to have a marine zoo close to where you live, you may not see an octopus. Ever. However, with TV, *Animal Planet,* the *Discovery Channel,* and Hollywood, it's likely that you know what an octopus looks like and also know that you don't want to meet one if it's hungry.

When Octopus appears in your life—and dreams certainly count— you're being told that some sort of camouflage is necessary to protect you from something. You don't even have to know what that *something* is; it's simply time to blend in with the crowd, to hang back, to become anonymous, faceless. Allow your inquisitive nature to lead you into unexplored areas.

Romance: The romantic prognosis for Octopus isn't very good. When you consider that both male and female die within months of mating and breeding, who needs it? However, if you're involved with someone and Octopus enters your life, then pay attention. Close attention. You're being warned that your partner may not be what you think he or she is. Beneath that cool exterior lies a clever predator, a changeling, and what you see is definitely not what you get. That said, this relationship can revolve primarily around sex, and if that's what you're looking for at this time, then go for it.

Finances: Be as flexible as you can be. You may have to diversify your assets, to camouflage them somehow. One friend of ours has multiple corporations where he had stashed his various assets, a perfectly legal maneuver, but infinitely confusing unless you really know what you're doing and can stay on top of it all. Don't tell other people what you earn.

Work/Career: Manual dexterity may be part of your daily work or necessary, somehow, to your career. This can include anything from carpentry and tool-making to using a computer to the arts. If you're a writer, consider using a pseudonym for a particular project. It's important now to diversify, to branch out, and to maintain secrecy about what you're doing.

Health: Maintain adaptability in all that you do and your health will remain vigorous and strong. However, you may want to have your eyes/vision checked. If your hand or arm goes numb at night, you should get checked for carpel tunnel syndrome. Surgery isn't called for, but alternative therapies might be. As a regular exercise routine, swimming is your best bet now. Meditation is beneficial for you.

Family: Octopus isn't a family or social creature. He's a loner. If you have an unresolved issue with a parent—and it's likely to be estrangement or abandonment—then now is the time to resolve it. Dive into the water of your own unconscious. Explore your dreams. Learn to request dreams that address particular issues. Go within.

Creativity: Your creative endeavors are achieved in solitude, by exploring who you are and how you came to be wherever you are. Use your life as fodder. Explore creative possibilities that involve manual dexterity and a flexible nature.

Spirituality: Forget, for the moment, that it's a stretch to equate an octopus with spirituality. Think of the animal's *qualities,* its *behavior,* the characteristics that are intrinsic to what it is. Once you do that, it's apparent that your spiritual path lies in adaptability, experimentation, and an exploration of your personal unconscious.

Brainstorming

Unless you work with marine animals, you're more likely to have an encounter in waking life with a porcupine than with an octopus. But an encounter with either one, in your waking or dreaming life, deserves deeper exploration. Here are some suggestions on how to enhance your connection to animals in this category:

Self-examination.

Where in your life do you need greater camouflage and protection? Or are you, perhaps, *too* camouflaged and protected? You might enlist the help of a trusted friend who can give you his or her perspective on these issues. As always, keeping a journal of your experiences and thoughts on this subject is helpful.

Books.

Numerous self-help books are on the market that explore questions such as these. You may want to start with Louise Hay's classic, *You Can Heal Your Life*. Even though Hay's approach is through the mind-body connection and the emotional basis of illness and disease, the wisdom in this book applies to all areas of life. Check the appendix for other books.

Volunteer work.

Volunteer at your local animal shelter or zoo. Not only is this a worthy cause, but you can learn a great deal about the camouflage and protections that certain animals use.

Take a research vacation.

There are many types of eco-tours offered these days. They range from bird and whale-watching trips to mountain treks through the Andes to marine trips. Research your options on the Internet.

Honoring Your Animal

To honor a porcupine or an octopus, two very different kinds of animals, you may want to consider the following suggestions:

Create effigies of your animal.

Whether you do this through sketching, sculpture or photography, the idea is the same. You are honoring your animal by placing its image in your personal areas. You are also reminding yourself about the true significance of your encounter with this camouflage animal.

Nature walks.

You probably won't see an octopus on your nature walks, but you might encounter a porcupine. Note details about the animal—how it moves, looks, acts, what it eats. Are there any similarities in behavior between you and the porcupine?

Education.

First, educate yourself about the animal. Know the facts. Then research its role in mythology, history, art. Become an expert. If possible, observe the animal in the wild. Teach others what you have learned.

12

Power

BEAR, LION

P ower: How we humans love that word. Whether it's personal power or the collective power of a nation, the power of a spiritual or political belief, or the power of a particular system (health care, the military, the pharmaceutical industry), power runs the world. On a global scale, power in the twenty-first century seems to be defined by who has the most money, the largest military, and the most oil. In this chapter, though, we're talking about personal power. What kind of power do we, as individuals, possess to write the script of our lives and to achieve our potential? How do we wield the power we own and how do we reclaim power we have disowned?

Recent events illustrate just how much power individuals can claim when they come together. Shortly before the U.S. invaded Iraq, several anti-war organizations galvanized millions of people worldwide to protest the invasion. They did it primarily through the Internet. It's estimated that ten million people protested worldwide, in more than a dozen countries.

When politicians began announcing their candidacy for the 2004 presidential race, not many people outside of Vermont had heard of Howard

Dean, that state's ex-governor. But within a few months, a grassroots campaign conducted primarily over the Internet had galvanized tremendous support for Dean, raising millions for his campaign.

This kind of individual power, though, isn't limited to protests or political campaigns. Throughout history, individuals with a singular vision have made significant contributions to society. The individual power we're talking about in this chapter begins within and then spills outward, touching other lives.

Many kinds of animals symbolize power simply because of their size (bears, lions, tigers, whales, gorillas, elephants); because of their defenses (venomous creatures); their speed (cheetahs, panthers); or a variety of other factors. But some of the most powerful animals are threatened or endangered and are covered in Chapter Fourteen. For this chapter, we've selected the bear and the lion.

BEAR

Myths, Folklore, Legends

Mythology and indigenous traditions are rich with bear lore. In Greek mythology, the story of bears begins with Zeus. As something of a philanderer, Zeus became infatuated with a young maiden named Kallisto. He disguised himself as Artemis, and then raped her. Kallisto was a member of the female hunting tribe headed by Artemis and all of them were virgins. So when Kallisto's pregnancy began to show, Artemis banished her from the tribe. Hera, Zeus's wife, saw her alone, vulnerable, and turned her into a bear. Kallisto still gave birth to her son, Akras, and he was turned over to Maia, the mother of Hermes, to raise.

Akras was brought up as a hunter and a mountain man and one day while he was out hunting, came face to face with a bear. He grabbed his spear to kill it, but Zeus intervened. The bear was Akras's mother and Zeus, rather than allow Akras to kill his own mother, swept them both up and placed them in the sky as the two bears, Ursa Major and Ursa Minor.

Native Americans also have stories that revolve around the Great Bear constellation. In these traditions, Bear represents the north and introspection.

When Bear Medicine Woman was still in her mother's womb, her father killed a bear, so she was born with the spirit of the bear. She's the origin of the Bear Medicine ceremony that invokes healing through the power of the bear.

In Finland in the sixteenth century, it was believed that when you ate the meat of a bear, you took on the animal's power and strength. Whenever a bear was killed, there was a feast in which the bear's head was placed in a position of honor. Even today in Finland, the bear is considered to be an intelligent creature with a soul that is actually that of a human being who lives in the forest.

In Norse legends, there were warriors called Berserks who dressed in bear skins and capitalized on the fear that ordinary people had of wild animals and of bears in particular. These warriors were, by any modern standard, complete nutcases who worked themselves into a frenzy by biting their shields and howling like animals. When enraged, they attacked trees or boulders and often killed their own people.

Some indigenous tribes didn't eat bear meat because they believed that bears were related to man. This belief undoubtedly came about because bears walk on two legs, just like man.

The bear is also associated with the goddess Diana, a lunar goddess still honored among pagans.

Facts and Trivia

The polar bear is the largest terrestrial carnivore and the only bear that is exclusively a meat eater. Its diet consists primarily of seals. The males often weigh over a thousand pounds. Despite the color of polar bears, they are very similar in appearance to other bears, with large, stocky bodies, short tails, and big heads. Most bears have poor eyesight and hearing that is only fair. But nature has equipped them with an acute sense of smell.

Bears are fond of ants and honey, but also eat bees, seeds, roots and berries. Grizzlies and Alaskan brown bears fish for salmon, and the panda bear—the big exception overall to the bear family—has a diet only of bamboo. But the bottom line is that most bears are opportunistic and will eat whatever they can, whenever they can.

The bear's reputation is largely undeserved. Although they're thought to be fierce and aggressive, they're generally solitary animals who prefer to roam undisturbed by humans. Even though we equate bears with fierceness, seeing them through the lens of our fear, wildlife biologist Lynn Rogers has used another approach. "Once I started looking at bears in terms of their fear, and interpreted all the things that used to scare me and interpreted those in terms of the bear's fear, it was easy to gain their trust," he says in *When Elephants Weep*.

Scientists who talk about the emotions of animals are often accused of anthropomorphism, but Rogers says, ". . .I think we miss the mark more by ignoring those emotions than by taking them into account."

Most bears reach sexual maturity in three to four years. During breeding season, pairs come together for a few days during the summer months. The gestation period is 220 days, then the cubs are born in the mother's den and are weaned at around eight months of age. They remain with the mother for a year and a half.

Some months ago, residents of southern Palm Beach County were put on the alert that a black bear was on the loose. Despite repeated efforts to trap it, the bear eluded capture and kept moving steadily northward, lumbering through the backyards of suburban homes. It traveled about twenty miles north and then westward to an equestrian community, where it was finally caught close to a local high school. Every day, residents who had sighted the bear were quoted in the local newspaper about their astonishment, awe, and delight. These people had come face to face with issues about personal power. The bear refused to conform to what it was *supposed* to do according to our rules and continued to roam free.

The bear was finally caught and released into the Florida Everglades.

Significance

Key Words: Power, strength, solitude, individuality

The Big Picture: When interpreting Bear's message, it's necessary to note the details of your experience. Did Bear appear in a dream? Did your experience happen in the wild? How did you feel? How did the bear act? It's possible that you need more solitude in your life so that you can save up your energy before moving ahead. Your power and strength at this time must begin within. Explore your own unconscious through dream work, meditation, and generally slow down the pace of your life.

Romance: Bear isn't an especially good harbinger for romance. But then again, you may not be in the mood for romance, either. For now, focus on yourself and trust that romance and love will unfold in its own time.

Finances: Any kind of work that you do in solitude is likely to benefit you financially. It's possible to earn money now while you travel. In fact, you should consider taking some time off to brainstorm, think, and reshuffle your financial planning.

Work/Career: Events may be moving swiftly at this time, so it's important that you center and ground yourself. Be sure about your priorities and goals. Don't team up with anyone else. Work alone, behind the scenes.

Health: You may have to change your diet and, again, the change depends on the type of bear you encountered. If it was a polar bear, then more meat and protein are called for. If it was a grizzly or Alaskan brown bear, more salmon should be added to your diet. If it was a panda—well, we don't recommend that you eat bamboo! However, you may want to consider a vegetarian diet for awhile.

Family: It's important to spend time with your children now. They may be at an age where they need more parental guidance or it may be that you need their youthful energy!

Creativity: Over the next eight months, you'll come up with several creative projects that are a natural outgrowth of solitude and reflection. To honor your creative voice now, it's important that you define your deepest dreams and hopes for the future—and then strive to achieve them.

Spirituality: It's time to get back to basics to find your spiritual center. Getting out into the wild will be beneficial and will help you gain perspective on how your spiritual beliefs are changing. Information about this spiritual path will come to you through dreams, meditation, and synchronicities.

LION

Myths, Folklore, Legends

The Sphinx. Chimera. The Griffin. Daniel in the lion's den. The lion in *The Wizard of Oz*. Richard the Lionhearted. Stories and myths about lions have endured since ancient times and generally, they all have the same theme: They depict the lion as the king of beasts, incomparably courageous.

In an ancient Egyptian mystery school, Sekhmet was the lion goddess, her name synonymous with power and might. In Hindu mythology, Durga, the fierce aspect of Shakti, is usually depicted riding on the back of a lion. In Syrian art, gods and goddesses stand on lions and lions often appeared in Palestinian, Assyrian, and Sumerian art.

The statue of the Sphinx is a lion with a human head. In some depictions of the Sphinx, it has wings. Most sphinxes symbolize a king in his appearance as the sun god. In many ceremonies, Egyptian priests wore the skins of lions, symbolic of the sun, which rules the sign of Leo—the lion.

Then, of course, there are the Hollywood myths and legends: *The Lion King, The Lion in Winter,* and C.S. Lewis's classic novel *The Lion, the Witch, and the Wardrobe.*

If you're still in doubt that the lion is the king of beasts, head over to your local zoo and sit for awhile in front of the lion's cage. In West Palm Beach, Florida, there's a fascinating zoo/park called Lion Country Safari, where you can drive through a massive park where lions, tigers, and dozens of other species roam free.

Facts and Trivia

When it comes down to carnivores, lions have it over almost every other animal on the planet. They are incapable of crushing their food because their teeth don't have any flat surfaces, just sharp spear-like blades. They have binocular vision and acute hearing. All cats are terrific tree climbers, but contrary to popular opinion, they don't look for trouble. They avoid confrontation.

The tiger is the largest cat of the pantherine family, which also includes the lion and the leopard. The tiger can weigh nearly seven hundred pounds and feeds on large prey. It's a solitary animal and a solitary hunter. A tiger's social unit usually consists of the female and her immediate cubs.

The lion is the most social of these cats, living in a pride that consists of five to fifteen adult females and their cubs, and anywhere from one to six male lions. They are social hunters who hunt as a team, surrounding a prey, stalking it, ambushing it. The male lion is always distinguishable from the female—he's the one with the gorgeous mane, whose tail swishes lazily in the warm sunlight, while the females do all the work. It seems that equality among the sexes hasn't quite reached the lion world.

Probably one of the most unusual stories about lions was told in Joy Adamson's book, *Born Free*, about a lion named Elsa whom Adamson and her husband raised and later released. The bonds between this woman and Elsa were apparently so strong that for years after her release, Elsa returned from the wild to visit Adamson and often had her mate and her children with her.

Recently, lions figured prominently in three different news items. Roy, of the Siegfried and Roy act in Las Vegas, was attacked by one of the lions he and Siegfried use in their act and is, as of this writing, still in critical condition. On the same day, a 400-pound lion was removed from an apartment in New York City, and Tiger Woods won another golf tournament. A friend e-mailed us and asked what all the lion symbolism meant.

The synchronicity of the three items appearing in the same twenty-four hours certainly grabs your attention. The stories address different levels of lion symbolism and the power these creatures represent. The Las Vegas incident points to the atavistic power of the animal itself. Despite the fact that Roy lived and slept with his lions, they are still wild animals living under abnormal conditions, who are expected to act in certain ways for the pleasure and entertainment of crowds. The attack was a reminder that lions aren't domesticated pets. A lion is not a golden retriever.

The second incident, the lion kept in a Manhattan apartment, apparently didn't entertain crowds, but was there for the owner's amusement. We have to wonder if the owner felt more powerful with the animal in his possession.

The third incident, with Tiger Woods, aptly illustrates how the power symbolized by this animal can be used in a personal way to achieve the extraordinary. Tiger Woods is a young black man who hasn't just cracked the ranks of pro golf, which is dominated by white men, but may be greater at the game than any of the famous white pro golfers.

Significance

Key Words: Courage, strength, instinct, group activities, personal power

The Big Picture: Where in your life do you require great courage now? How can your group associations help you to achieve your full potential? If you're a man, you may be entering a period in your life where women or yin energy will prove to be important to you. Or, you may have to draw on the feminine side of your nature to achieve or realize a dream. If you're a woman, it may be time for you to withdraw into the depths of your unconscious and explore what's there. Eventually, you'll be called upon to bring this knowledge to the surface and impart it to others. If you're a man, it's time to get off your duff and take charge.

Romance: Animal magnetism. A sexual relationship may sweep you into desires you didn't even know you had. Your partner may not be the soul mate you've been hoping for, but he or she is a necessary step in that direction.

Finances: Don't depend on advisors to make your financial decisions. Be decisive, keep your business to yourself, and listen to your instincts. A woman may prove helpful or you may depend more on your own intuition. If you're male, it's time to take charge of what you earn and what you spend and to balance the books.

Work/Career: You're entering a powerful period of your professional life. Stealth is important. Your group associations, your network of acquaintances and friends, are helpful now. Don't lose sight of what you're trying to achieve.

Define your goals and go for it! Don't let fear or self-doubt hold you back or prevent you from exploring areas that interest you.

Health: It's time to establish an exercise routine. Forget the gym. You need contact with the outdoors. It's possible that you may partner with someone else for a daily walk or run. The point here isn't how far or how fast you walk or run. It's that you do it regularly, daily. You may benefit from yoga for your joints and flexibility.

Family: If you're a woman with young children, you get help from a woman—a mother, sister, relative, friend—who can be with your children when you're not at home. If you're a man, it may be time for you to get more involved with your kids and family life. It also may be time to pitch in and help more around the house. Equality may not exist in the pride, but if want your partnership to last, equality better come to your house!

Creativity: Get to work. Whatever your creative passion, now is the time to act. Set aside time each day to work exclusively on your creative interests. Long walks may help to stimulate your creative adrenaline.

Spirituality: If you've been living your spiritual beliefs in the abstract, now is the time to test them out in your daily life. If you believe that you live in a safe universe—but have three dead bolt locks on your door, an infallible security system, and carry a weapon, what kind of message is this sending to your higher self? If you're a Buddhist who beats your kids, a professed vegetarian who still eats meat occasionally, then what message does this send to yourself and others?

Brainstorming

Personal power is an odd term. What, exactly, does it really mean? To us, it means the ability and opportunity to achieve your emotional, physical, spiritual, and psychic potential. If you've had an experience with a bear, lion, or any other animal associated with power, then pay very close attention and ask yourself two questions. Are you in need of personal power? Or are you exerting too much power over the lives of others? In both instances, apply our definition of personal power.

Now apply both questions to animals—wild and domesticated, farm and companions. How many animals of your acquaintance have the opportunity to achieve their potential? Do you regard the animals who share your life as *your* property? Do you declaw your cats, prevent them from going outside, or scold them when they miss the litter box? Do you play with your dogs? Walk them? Feed them food they like? Do you take them to the doctor when they're ill? Or are your animal companions simply there for *your* enjoyment?

One woman we know adopted a cat from the animal shelter only to discover the animal had a tumor on one of its legs. Instead of taking the cat to the vet, she made her son save his allowance for the surgery. During the time the son was saving his money, the woman blithely spent several thousand to rent a vacation condo and several hundred dollars for a new dog. When the son finally had the money saved for the surgery, the vet discovered that the tumor was malignant and gave the cat only a few months to live.

A strange synchronicity grew out of this chain of events. The woman herself was diagnosed with cancer.

All too often, we fail to recognize the connections between the states of our lives and the kinds of experiences we attract—and the way we live our lives. Every component is intimately connected to every other component. It's rather like the Butterfly Effect—that the flutter of a butterfly's wings in China may create a tornado on the other side of the world—except that it applies to human life.

If you discover that you're exerting too much control over the lives of others (humans and animals), then perhaps it's time to back off and get more into the flow of things. If you've discovered that what you need is more personal power, then get busy creating the conditions and circumstances that will allow you more opportunities for achieving your potential.

Honoring Your Animal

To honor your power animal, decide which of the questions in the "Brainstorming" section apply to you. Then take one, decisive action each day for the next week or two weeks or month, whatever time frame you feel comfortable with, that illustrates your intent to change. You might consider creating a blueprint for action, with specific steps you can follow to either gain more personal power—or to release the power you exert over others.

13

Independence
and Solitude

DOMESTIC CAT, IGUANA

There are undoubtedly many kinds of animals that would fit in this chapter. The aardvark and the wild pig are two that come to mind immediately. While you may encounter a wild pig at some point in your life, you probably won't meet up with an aardvark.

We chose the domestic cat and the iguana for this chapter. Both are solitary and independent creatures and are also common animal companions. But before we discuss these two animals, let's explore what we mean by independence and solitude.

Even if you're a gregarious, social person, there are times in your life when you need solitude to recharge and to explore who you are. Independence is a trickier word, though. When we're teens, we seek independence from our parents and family. When we're adults, we are (hopefully) independent beings who establish our own lives, families, careers, passions, and interests. But if you look at the dictionary definition of the word, independence means "not depending on another thing for validity or on another person for one's opinion; unwilling to be under obligation to others."

That definition, as anyone with a feline companion will tell you, certainly fits the nature of the domestic cat. It also fits the nature of the iguana. It may even fit you. And yet, regardless of how independent you consider yourself to be, there will always be times in your life when you need other people. Your car breaks down on the highway. What do you do? You call AAA or a friend or you call home.

By independence and solitude, we don't mean your intrinsic nature. We're talking about transitory qualities.

DOMESTIC CAT

Myths, Folklore, Legends

The cat's appearance in mythology and folklore is ancient. Bastet was the Egyptian cat-headed goddess, around whom a great cat cult grew. Initially, she was a solar deity, but once the Greeks got into the act, she became associated with Artemis and became a lunar goddess. She was portrayed as either a wild desert cat or as a lioness. Not until around 1000 B.C. did she become associated with the domesticated cat.

The cult of Bastet was centered in the temple of Bubastis, which was written about by the historian Herodotus. He described the festivities that took place in honor of this goddess. Since Bastet was thought to incarnate as a cat, these animals were regarded as household deities. Due to the popularity of the cult, cats were depicted in every conceivable material, from papyrus to stone and bronze. At one time, there were even cat cemeteries laid out along the banks of the Nile.

Cats, of course, figure prominently in *Grimm's Fairy Tales* and children's writers have always used them to illustrate morals or principles. Probably one of the most famous children stories is Dr. Seuss's *The Cat in the Hat*. Hollywood hasn't been immune, either. From *That Darn Cat* to *Incredible Journey* and *Lady and the Tramp,* these animals have always held a prominent role in human life.

Facts and Trivia

In the U.S., the number of cats as animal companions is around seventy-three million. Nearly thirty-five million households have at least one cat. More than half of cat owners have female cats and twenty percent of the total were adopted from animal shelters. Eighty percent of all cats are spayed or neutered.

In case you're interested in how dogs as animal companions measure up statistically to cats, the figure stands at around sixty-eight million.

The ancient Egyptians were the first people to tame cats, which they used to control—what else?—rodents and other pests. Phoenician cargo ships probably brought the first domesticated cats to Europe, and then the pilgrims later brought the cat to North America.

Physiologically, cats are intriguing creatures. Their eyesight and hearing far surpass our own. They need only one sixth of the light we do to see because their eyes have extra layers of cells that absorb light. They can hear sounds at higher frequencies than we do and can rotate their ears independently. In the scent department, they're far better endowed than we are. While we have between five and twenty million olfactory cells in our noses, cats have anywhere from sixty to eighty million. They also have a special scent organ on the roof of their mouth that analyzes smells. The kittens in a cat's litter can all have different fathers, an attribute that explains why kittens in a litter often show striking differences in coloring and size.

The psychic bonds between cats and their human companions is well known among people who own these animals. Millie owned a cat named Cinnamon, often referred to as "My Cin," a stray who came to her house while her mother, Florence, was living with her. Cinnamon refused to leave even after being told several times that she was not wanted.

One morning after Millie opened the door to enter, Cinnamon quickly jumped across the threshold of the house, then ran and jumped on Florence's lap. In that moment she stole Florence's heart and the tri-color calico was there to stay.

She became a constant companion and was extremely sensitive when Florence became ill and was ultimately bedridden. When Florence was particularly ill, Cinnamon would jump up on the bed and lie across her to give her warmth. At other times she would stay close by, lying at the foot of the bed and comforting Florence just by her presence.

When Florence died, Cinnamon stayed on with Millie, who knows her mother returns in spirit to love and guide her through lonely or sick periods of her life. A magnet that hangs in Millie's home states: "Cats Are in Charge Here."

These psychic bonds between people and their animal companions are now an area of scrutiny. In *Dogs That Know When Their Owners Are Coming Home,* biologist Rupert Sheldrake has documented hundreds of stories about dogs, cats, horses, reptiles, and birds, who seem to share inexplicable bonds with their owners. These bonds, of course, aren't inexplicable to people who shares their lives with animals. As any cat owner will tell you, cats are psychic!

Significance

Key Words: Independence, solitude, mystery, nocturnal

The Big Picture: When Cat comes into your life, it's time to kick back, detach, and spend more time alone. Your sleeping habits may change, too, with longer periods of sleep during the day, which leaves nighttime hours open for creative work, exploration, or wherever your passions and interests lead you. Whatever you perceive during the night will be particularly important to you. Your clarity will be greater. There's a timing device with cats, the same as the gestation period for their kittens: sixty-two to sixty-five days.

Romance: You're cruising, prowling, looking for action (maybe in the wrong places), and whoever you meet during this period in your life is sure to ignite new emotions and thoughts. The relationship may not last long, but it will be important in the overall scheme of your life because of what you learn. If nothing else, this person is mysterious, strange, and seductive.

Finances: You may take a part-time job for awhile, perhaps a night job, to supplement your income or to earn extra money for something special. It's also possible that over the next two months, new opportunities appear for investments or that you get a raise.

Work/Career: If you've ever considered becoming self-employed, now is the time to work toward that goal. Lay your groundwork, do your homework, and keep your plans to yourself.

Health: Your diet and nutrition may need attention and you should get your eyes and hearing checked. In the diet department, perhaps you need more protein now and should consider taking supplemental herbs. Try eating more fish, particularly deep-water fish like sardines and salmon. An exercise routine is important at this time. Don't worry about what it is, as long as you enjoy it and do it regularly. Avoid aspirin or its derivatives and try catnaps to replenish your energy.

Family: Children—your own or someone else's—figure prominently in your life now. They stimulate your curiosity and innocence and you, in turn, guide them with your wisdom. Your family may include getting a new animal companion. Head over to the local animal shelter and save a life!

Creativity: As you begin to alternate your sleep patterns, it will be easier to remember your dreams, a source of inspiration and creative fodder. Try to do your creative work at night for awhile and to use symbolism and archetypes as springboards for ideas. You may also want to read some of the newer animal books that have been published recently. One that's particularly good is *A Cat Named Darwin,* by William Jordan. The subtitle of the book says it all: *How a Stray Cat Changed a Man into a Human Being.*

Spirituality: Your spiritual path now is enriched through contact with nature, animals, and investigations into mysteries.

IGUANA

Myths, Folklore, Legends

Much of the mythology and folklore about lizards comes from countries with warm climates.

Among the Aborigines, Wati-kutjara are lizard men who came from the Dreamtime. Their totem is the iguana. They created ceremonial objects that they gave to the Aborigines and also created trees and plants.

The Polynesians had a lizard god endowed with magical powers. In African mythology, Tchue was a hero of the Bushmen. He brought the gift of fire to the people and at various times was depicted as a lizard, a bird, and an elephant.

In Mayan mythology, the great god Kukulcan was a creator and a god of resurrection and reincarnation. His origins in Toltec myth have him emerging from the ocean and returning to it again after he had brought the Toltec just about everything that mattered—fishing, the calendar, and agriculture. Kukulcan was eventually merged with the Aztec myth of Quetzalcoatl and one of his attributes was lizard—or fire.

Among the Bakairi Indians of South America, Evaki was the goddess of night and day. She owned a pot with a lid on it and whenever she lifted the lid, the sun came out; when she put the lid back on the pot, the sun couldn't be seen anymore. Evaki supposedly stole sleep from the lizard's eyes, which is why a lizard's eyes bulge!

So depending on which myth you're reading, the lizard is associated with Dreamtime, the sun, life, death and resurrection, and creation.

Facts and Trivia

As our hunger increases for ever more exotic pets, iguanas are emerging as one of the favorites and may be the most popular of all lizards in the pet trade.

They come from the family Iguanids and are related to the chameleon. They are found mostly in Central and South America, but also on the islands of the Caribbean, the Galapagos, and on islands in the South Pacific.

In the wild, iguanas can reach six feet or more in length and a female can produce more than seventy eggs. They lay their eggs on the ground, in buried nests, and when the hatchlings emerge, they do so en masse. Green iguanas are vegetarians who, in the wild, eat plants, fruit, leaves, even grass. When kept as pets, it's recommended that they be fed green beans, turnip greens, parsley, grape leaves, snow peas, mulberry leaves, and cilantro.

Iguanas are diurnal—active during the day—so their association in some cultures with dreams is rather curious. Perhaps it has to do with the long hours that they laze in the sun, their eyes half closed. When kept as pets, the right lighting is essential. Fluorescent and incandescent lighting are recommended, as well as full spectrum bulbs, so that the iguana is able to produce vitamin D3. If they don't get enough proper lighting, then they can't absorb calcium, and they will develop a bone disease.

Adult iguanas have a parietal or median eye on the tops of their heads. It doesn't see in the normal sense of the word, but it senses light and dark and may be used in some way to detect predators that are above them.

The only marine iguana in existence lives on the Galapagos Islands off the coast of Ecuador. They're the only iguana dependent on the marine environment and eat mostly marine algae. They have a special nasal gland that allows them to get rid of excess salt that they ingest from swimming and eating marine algae. The marine iguanas aren't as solitary as their green cousins; they aren't green, either. They're black, which absorbs the heat more easily, and they often bask on the rocks by the hundreds.

There's some speculation about how these huge iguanas reached the islands, since the Galapagos have never been connected to any land mass. It's believed that they hitched rides on floating vegetation.

The green iguana reaches sexual maturity around the age of two. Iguanas bob their heads when they're interested in each other and may extend the flap of skin under their throats, in much the same way that other lizards do. The male mounts the female and bites her on the back of the neck, presumably to hold her still. The gestation period is between seventy and ninety days.

Green iguanas aren't recommended as pets for kids. They can be aggressive if they aren't handled properly. And, let's face it, wouldn't you be somewhat cranky confined to a terrarium?

Significance

Key Words: Independence, solitude, past-life connections

The Big Picture: Whether Iguana or Lizard has appeared, the result is pretty much the same. You're in for a period of solitude and should tend to your business, whatever it is, and not worry about what other people are doing. Anyone you meet during this time may be connected to you through past lives and there could be some karma (either good or bad) to work out. There's a timing built in with this animal: 70 to 90 days.

Romance: You're soaking up the rays. A knockout man or woman sits down next to you. You glance at each other. Something happens, and you both feel it. That's the kind of experience you can expect. It's visceral, chemical, an immediate knowing. It doesn't mean this person is your soul mate, although he or she could be. What it *does* mean, however, is that you've come together at this place and time for a particular purpose.

Finances: Time to chill out, kick back, and maybe take a vacation. Even if you feel you can't afford a vacation, get in your car and drive somewhere secluded, into the country, into the mountains, to the beach, wherever you can spend some time alone. And while you're alone, re-think your financial strategies and how you're earning your living.

Work/Career: This category is closely connected with the one on finances. For most of us, after all, our work is how we pay the bills. So get away from the grind, take a few days off, and try to figure out what you would like to do with the rest of your life.

Health: Try a vegetarian diet for awhile or at least add more vegetables and fruits to your diet. Make that *fresh* fruit and veggies. Watch your intake of salt and make sure you have enough calcium in your diet. If you're a woman over the age of fifty, take calcium supplements. Make sure you're getting enough sun, too. If you live in the north and it's winter, you might consider using a UV lamp.

Family: If you have a family of your own, then it may be time for a family vacation—just you, your spouse, the kids. No friends, no relatives. Just the family *unit*. In fact, if Iguana or Lizard shows up in your life, you may want to consider a trip to the Galapagos!

Creativity: At this time, your creativity is at its highest peak during the daylight hours. But because of Lizard's association with Aboriginal Dreamtime, start paying attention to your dreams, try to recall them, to learn the symbols of your unconscious. During the day, you may want to nap frequently.

Spirituality: Read, reflect, think, travel, spend time alone. Get to know yourself first.

Brainstorming

To deepen your connection with animals that represent independence and solitude, it would be advantageous for you to engage in activities that promote those qualities. Start with small things—go to a movie alone, eat alone in a restaurant—and progress to larger things, like traveling alone or making important decisions separate from a parent, spouse, or partner. You might also spend more time observing and studying your cat or iguana. If you do this with patience and sincere intent, it won't be long before you're able to interpret your companion's "language."

Trish's family has three cats, each with a distinct personality. Whiskers, the alpha male, was born feral in their neighborhood and when he was six or seven weeks old, Trish, her daughter, and a neighbor, brought all the kittens to the MacGregor porch. They were afraid that if the kittens grew up and roamed the neighborhood, they would end up at animal control and might be euthanized. So the plan was that the kittens would live with the MacGregors until they could be placed in good homes. Whiskers ended up as a permanent member of the family—and is no longer feral!

One night not long after the kittens had been taken from the mother, she appeared at the porch door, making such a pathetic and heartbreaking sound that everyone in the house rushed to the porch to see what was going on. And right then, the mother cat lifted her paw to the screen, as if reaching out to her kittens, and made that sound again that everyone understood as, *Why did you take away my babies?*

The next day, a neighbor adopted the mother cat, which was also feral, and after that, she never came around to the porch again. But the poignancy of that moment endures.

Iguanas may not be as expressive in that sense as cats, but anyone who has worked with them or observed them will tell you they have distinct personalities and quirks every bit as endearing as any other animal. With time and patience, it's possible to learn the language of any solitary animal.

Honoring Your Animal

If the animal you're honoring lives in your home, honoring it can be as simple and straightforward as treating it the same way you treat anyone you love and care for. Do special things for your animal companion—get catnip for your cats, fresh fruits for your iguana, spend time with the animals. All of this seems obvious, but how many cat owners do you know who confine the animal to a particular area of the house, declaw it, and don't allow it to go outside? How many cat owners do you know who treat their animals as if they were merely property?

If the animal you're honoring doesn't live with you, then you might want to consider these suggestions:

Volunteer at an animal shelter.

If the shelter where you volunteer employs euthanasia, speak out against it. If possible, adopt animals that are about to be euthanized or help place them in good homes.

Volunteer for a pet rescue organization.

Many of these organizations are manned almost entirely by volunteers who do it out of love for animals.

Educate others.

Put up a website on animals that educates others about animal companions. Speak to elementary school classes. Small children who learn early on that animals aren't on the planet just for us, and that they have a right to freedom and life, tend to be more compassionate as adults. Promote awareness in children through example.

14

Endangered Animals

So many animals are endangered that it's beyond the capacity of this book to even list them all. What we've done, instead, is to select endangered animals from a cross section of species and provide a brief description for each animal to illustrate the quality it embodies that we are in danger of losing. In some instances, we speculate about what the extinction of this animal could portend for us in terms of future events.

Take the dodo bird. This strange creature was discovered in 1507 and was extinct by 1680. It lived on the island of Mauritius, east of Madagascar in the Indian Ocean, and hardly qualified as the cutest bird on the block. Its black bill looked as crinkled as tissue paper, had a tinge of red in it, and was oddly shaped. The bird was ash gray, with wings that were little more than useless stubs. It weighed about fifty pounds and was thought to be the descendant of pigeons that had flown to the island centuries before.

The dodo had lived an isolated existence on the island, so when Portuguese explorers came ashore, it greeted them with an almost childlike innocence. The sailors misinterpreted its innocence and lack of fear as stupidity and called it "Dodo," a Portuguese word that roughly translates as simpleton. The sailors killed the dodos in droves for food and subsequently introduced pigs, cats, rats, and monkeys that preyed on the birds as well.

The sixteenth century was a time of brutality and ignorance—the witchcraft trials, the beginning of the slaughter of the North American Indian, the Great Plague of London that killed nearly 70,000 people, the persecution of Galileo—and that's just for starters. Perhaps the extinction of the dodo bird signaled the loss of our own childlike innocence in a time when we needed it most.

Another bird that met with extinction was the North American passenger pigeon. Unlike the dodo, however, it was found all over the continent and at one time was possibly the most abundant bird in the world. In good breeding years, flocks reached astonishing numbers. In 1866, a flight of birds moving north from the U.S. was three hundred miles long and a mile wide and went on for fourteen hours.

So what, exactly, happened to these birds? They were exterminated, slaughtered relentlessly—shot, trapped, and poisoned by the millions. During a breeding season in Michigan in 1874, 25,000 passenger pigeons were killed daily, amounting to nearly a million in a single month. By 1880, the bird was closing in on extinction. The last one died in 1914 in the Cincinnati Zoo.

The timing of the bird's death in a historical context may hold clues to what its extinction portended. World War I began the same year that the last passenger pigeon died. By 1918, eight and a half million people had been killed, twenty-one million had been wounded, and nearly eight million were POWs or missing. In 1929, fifteen years after the last passenger pigeon died, the stock market crashed, ushering in the worst depression the U.S. has ever seen. In 1932, Austrian-born Adolph Hitler was given his German citizenship. In 1933, Hitler was granted dictatorial powers and the first concentration camps were erected by the Nazis. By 1945, almost six million people had been exterminated and many millions more confined to prisons.

World-renowned British biologist Rupert Sheldrake hypothesizes the existence of morphic fields that guide and shape all chemical, physical, and biological systems, at every level of complexity. These fields produce a resonance which, over time, builds up a kind of collective memory within a species.

In *Presence of the Past,* he writes, "The morphic fields of any particular organism, say a sunflower plant, are shaped by influences from previous generations of sunflowers." Or dogs. Or cats. Or man. In other words, what one generation learns is stored in the morphic field of that species and the next generation is born with that knowledge or skill or set of behaviors.

In 1921 in Southampton, England, a Blue Tit bird was observed opening a milk bottle by tearing open the aluminum flap. The habit was observed at regular intervals between 1930 and 1947, in eleven species of tits. The habit accelerated as time went on and eventually appeared in other countries—even though tits generally don't travel more than a few miles from their breeding place. In Holland, milk bottles pretty much vanished during the war and became common again around 1947 or 1948. It's doubtful that any tits who had learned this habit before the war would still be alive, but attacks on the bottles started up again. While some scientists believed that instinctive behavior explained this phenomenon, Sheldrake disagreed. "Habits acquired by some animals can facilitate the acquisition of the same habits by other, similar animals, even in the absence of any known means of connection or communication."

If Sheldrake is right, then our future generations should be born understanding the importance of each species in the delicate balance of nature on the planet, and perhaps conservation won't be such a tragic struggle. Perhaps extinctions will become a thing of the past.

The Endangered Species Act of 1973

The Endangered Species Act was passed by Congress in 1973. Once a plant or an animal makes the list, it receives federal protection. But getting on the list is often the most difficult challenge. The listing program follows a strict legal procedure to determine whether a species should be listed, which is based on the degree of threat.

The act defines *endangered* as a species that "is in danger of extinction throughout all or a significant portion of its range."

A *threatened* species is "one that is likely to become endangered in the foreseeable future."

As of September 1, 2003, there were 1072 animals species that were endangered or threatened worldwide. This includes mammals, birds, reptiles, amphibians, fish, clams, snails, insects, arachnids, and crustaceans. In the U.S., as of October 17, 2003, 516 U.S. species of animals are listed, with another 27 species of animals currently proposed for listing. Another 117 species of animals are candidates for listing. Species on the list include the largest animal on the planet—the blue whale—to the miniscule thickshell pond snail. At this rate, by 2025, the Earth could lose one fifth of all species known today.

Aquatic species are often overlooked. But to date, one third of the U.S. fish species, two thirds of the crayfish species, and nearly three quarters of the mussel species are in trouble.

Every day, nearly a hundred species of plant and animals become extinct. The U.S. Fish and Wildlife Service has a website that includes all these statistics, plus updates and newsletters and a virtual treasure trove of information on endangered animals: see www.fws.gov/

The organization that lists endangered animals is the Red Data Book of the International Union for the Conservation of Nature.

ENDANGERED MAMMALS

Bison (Buffalo)

At one time, fifty to sixty million bison thundered across the American plains. They were great migrators and traveled in massive herds, creating what was probably one of the most astonishing spectacles ever seen.

Even though the Plains Indians depended on the bison for food, they didn't threaten its existence. They revered the animal as a symbol of abundance. Many of the Plains tribes believed the buffalo was associated with feminine magic, and women used ritual and dance to bring the buffalo closer to the village. Among the Blackfoot, a women's society called the Ma'toki or Buffalo Cows performed in a sundance that opened the summer hunt.

The arrival of the Europeans, however, began the path toward near extinction, when millions of bison were slaughtered for their meat and hides. The tongues were considered to be a great delicacy and quite often the bison were killed just for that, with the rest of the carcass left to rot. The animals were also killed for sport, with train passengers taking shots at them from the windows and so-called heroes of the West bragging about how many bison they had killed. Buffalo Bill boasted that he had killed over four thousand bison in a single year.

By 1884, the population of bison had been reduced to just 800 bison. Reserves were established and the remaining bison were protected. Today, thanks to protection and management, there are about 40,000 bison in refuges.

These massive animals can weigh up to a ton, have shaggy fur, a hump on the back, and large heads.

Significance: Although still endangered, the bison numbers are rising, perhaps signaling a more open attitude in the Western world toward the study of feminine energy, shamanism, and the role of spiritual beliefs in daily life. But until the bison is off the endangered list, the power of the feminine will still be suspect and denigrated in non-Western societies.

Blue Whale

The blue whale is the largest mammal on the planet. The male can grow to more than eighty feet in length and weighs over 110 tons. Females are larger than the males and weigh in around 150 tons. On land, an animal this size would be crushed by its own weight.

These mammals are found in every ocean and make lengthy migrations every winter and summer. During the winter, they mate and calve in tropical or temperate waters and then feed in polar waters during the summer. Blue whales in the northern hemisphere travel north to the Arctic to feed, and the whales in the southern hemisphere travel to the Antarctic.

Calves are born at intervals of two to three years and gestation is about a year. Calves are hefty at birth—twenty-three to twenty-seven feet long—and weigh three tons. They nurse for seven or eight months and are weaned when they reach fifty-two feet in length and weigh about twenty-three tons. During the nursing period, calves consume about a hundred gallons of the mother's milk and gain 200 pounds a day or about eight pounds an hour.

Blue whales usually travel in pairs, but sometimes travel in loosely defined groups of fifty to sixty whales. They're fast swimmers, capable of reaching speeds of thirty miles an hour, but generally cruise at around twelve. Their size and speed kept them relatively safe from early whalers, who used hand harpoons. All that changed in 1868, however, when a Norwegian invented an exploding harpoon gun. This invention turned the whaling industry upside down, and, after 1900, whalers focused on blue whales, which could yield up to 120 barrels of oil, and thousands of these creatures were slaughtered. The slaughter peaked in 1931 with 29,000 blue whales killed in a single season.

The exact numbers of blue whales alive today are, at best, an estimate: about ten to twelve thousand.

Significance: In the larger sense, the U.S. military would be wise to learn the blue whale lesson—that might and size don't necessarily ensure safety and survival. On a personal level, the endangered blue whale symbolizes lack of communication, which lies at the root of most of the problems in the world.

Elephant

The elephant is included in Chapter Six, but it makes an appearance here as well.

Of the three species of elephants—African, Indian, and Asiatic—the African elephant is the largest. There are an estimated 200,000 African elephants left on the planet, but the animal is endangered because it doesn't reproduce quickly enough to replace those elephants that are slaughtered in illegal hunting. It's estimated that 70,000 elephants are slaughtered annually just to supply ivory from tusks. Poachers are indiscriminate hunters and often shoot elephants who are in their reproductive prime. Elephants are also at risk because human habitation encroaches on their habitat, so more and more elephants are confined to a particular area and deplete the vegetation.

Most of an elephant's day—up to twenty hours—is spent feeding or moving toward a food or water source. The rest of their day is spent bathing, playing, sleeping, and reproducing. To maintain their massive bodies, they consume as much as 330 pounds of food and 30 gallons of water a day. They're strictly herbivores—living off branches, twigs, leaves, grass foliage, fruit, wood pulp, and grasses.

These giants live in matriarchal family units that consist of the alpha female and five to ten other elephants. Females can't breed until they're sexually mature, which begins around the age of fourteen, and are pregnant for nearly two years. The calves are tended to by all the females in the herd. Males strike out on their own when they're mature, around the age of thirteen, and sometimes form bachelor herds with other males. Adult bulls join the female herds only when a female is in estrus.

Jeffrey Moussaieff Masson and Susan McCarthy have brought to light the emotional lives of elephants and other animals in *When Elephants Weep*. They relate one particularly poignant story about a herd that traveled slowly because one of the females was carrying a small calf that had been dead for several days. Whenever she stopped to eat or drink, she set the calf on the ground. Even though she traveled slowly, the rest of the herd waited for her.

"This suggests that animals, like people, act on feelings as such, rather than solely for purposes of survival," write Masson and McCarthy. "A single example such as this one, no matter how well documented, may not change the entire evolutionary paradigm for feelings, but it raises questions that biologists have to face."

This isn't an isolated case. Read the story in Chapter Six!

It seems that the questions biologists have yet to face are also questions that humans need to confront—that animals feel physical and emotional pain, just as we do.

Significance: On a universal level, the endangered African elephant symbolizes the serious fissures in family and social structures as well as the risk of being female in certain countries. While Western women have made tremendous strides in equality, women in other countries have not been permitted the same freedom. Recently, a Nigerian woman faced death by stoning because she'd had a child out of wedlock—a child brought about by rape.

On a personal level, this endangered giant reminds us that in a transient world, where most of us have long since left the geographical areas of our childhood, we risk losing family roots and may find it difficult to make lifelong friends.

Key Deer

The Florida Keys are made up of a string of islands that stretch from Miami to Key West, a distance of about a hundred miles. Each island has its own peculiar mystique and interesting wildlife. But Big Pine Key is unique because it's an official refuge for the Key deer.

This species is the smallest of all American deer. It resembles a white-tailed deer, but its legs are stockier, and its skull is wider. Its main food source is red mangrove, but it eats a variety of others plants as well. It breeds all year, but the breeding season peaks in September and October. Only one fawn a year is born to females.

In the eighteenth century, these deer were so abundant that they were a major food source. By 1939, they were endangered and by the 1950s, the estimated Key deer population was twenty-five—and that was long before cars became the primary culprit in their deaths. Between 1980 and 1992, nearly 600 Key deer were killed by cars.

Today, the Key deer population is estimated to be about 800.

Significance: We are in danger of losing our humanity.

Manatees

The manatee or sea cow looks like a prehistoric creature. In fact, these creatures have existed since the Eocene epoch some fifty-seven million to thirty-seven million years ago and are thought to be related to the elephant. Only four species of sea cows exist today—one dugong and three manatees. A fifth species, Steller's sea cow, became extinct in the eighteenth century, within thirty years of its discovery. The cause? Man.

The sea cow crawls at the pace of molasses along ocean or river bottoms using its two front flippers and pumps its horizontal tails up and down to move itself forward. It has small eyes, its ears are tiny openings located just behind the eyes, and two nostrils are located on the upper surface of the snout. The nostrils are equipped with skin flaps that keep water out while the sea cow is underwater.

These guys are large—from ten to thirteen feet long—and can weigh as much as 3,300 pounds. The West African manatees are somewhat smaller, while the Amazonian manatees and dugongs are about ten feet long and weigh up to 500 pounds.

The largest concentration of West Indian manatees, about three thousand of them, are found in Florida, where the temperature of the water is just about perfect for them. They sometimes migrate as far north as the Carolinas or as far west as Louisiana during the summer. In the wild, they live between fifty and sixty years.

Manatees are herbivores and feed on a variety of aquatic plant life. They also eat floating palm fruits and have been known to use low-hanging branches to drag themselves out of the water and onto land to reach vegetation. They seem to have a built-in detector for plants with natural toxins like spatterdock and waterpennywort. In a single day, the manatee consumes between five and nine percent of its body weight in food.

Gestation for calves is about a year. Female manatees are attentive mothers and communicate with their young through chirps and high-pitched squeaks and squeals. A calf rarely ventures far from Mom and often rides on her back through the first eighteen months of its life, until it is weaned. Calves are three to four feet long when born and weigh about seventy pounds. The calf tends to be quite vocal and starts making noises as soon as it's born.

Many manatees have telltale scars on their backs from collisions with boats, the primary threat to the West Indian Manatee. Between 2000 and 2002, in Florida alone, 903 manatees were killed; twenty-three percent of them by boats. The bottom line threat to manatees, of course, is the rapid development along the Florida coastline, which has resulted in the loss and degradation of their habitat.

Significance: Our world is now moving so quickly that there's hardly time to process what we experience. As a species and as individuals, we're in danger of forgetting how to pause and smell the roses!

Red Wolf

Wolves: There's something almost mystical about them. Their howls, their swiftness, their sleek beauty. At one time, the red wolf was found throughout the southeastern U.S. from Pennsylvania to Florida and as far west as Texas. Yet, in 1980, red wolves were officially declared extinct in the wild, when the U.S. Fish and Wildlife Service rounded up fewer than twenty of them to breed in captivity.

Seven years later, the breeding program had been successful enough. Today, 155 captive red wolves live in 37 breeding facilities in the U.S. The red wolves that were reintroduced into the Great Smoky Mountains in 1991 were relocated in 1998 because there wasn't enough food. But the red wolf is testament that breeding and reintroduction programs can work.

The red wolf is about the size of a large dog. Adult males weigh sixty to eighty pounds and females weigh between forty and sixty pounds. They're smaller than their gray wolf cousins.

This wolf is shy and secretive. It breeds once a year in late winter and six to eight pups are born about two months later. It hunts alone or in small packs, and its diet consists of small mammals like rabbits and rodents. But it has been known to eat insects, berries, and even deer.

The wolf pack is a complex hierarchy with well-defined rules. The pack is ruled by the alpha male and he and the alpha female usually mate for life. Each member of the pack understands its position relative to every other member of the pack.

"A wolf pack is a wholly devoted extended family," write Jim and Jamie Dutcher, authors of *Wolves at Our Door*. "It is bound together by a common purpose and, at times, it seems, a common mind." This is noticeable during a hunt, the authors write, when the young learn by watching. "They witness how the adults change their strategy according to conditions and type of prey. They learn how the hunters handle each different situation: what to do when the prey dashes for open ground or jumps into a river or turns to defend itself." By the time the pups are ready to hunt, they know exactly what to do. "It is almost eerie how a pack can appear to be of a single mind."

This extended family is caring and solicitous toward wolf pups, and in the event the parents aren't able to care for the pups, another wolf will adopt them. The Dutchers believe that the bond a wolfpack shares with its family "is certainly as strong as the bond a human being has to his or her family."

Its endangered status has come about because of illegal hunting and habitat loss through development. Recently, we received an e-mail from Defenders of Wildlife, alerting us to the barbaric practice of aerial gunning of wolves in Alaska. In a single month, 91 wolves were shot, with plans to kill 80% of the wolves in an 8,000 square mile area of Alaska.

"Aerial hunters gun the wolves down from the air or chase them to exhaustion in the deep snow, then land and shoot them point-blank. Under the pretense of boosting moose populations for hunters, aerial hunters can even kill pregnant females and wolf pups. Numerous scientific studies show that wolves are actually beneficial to the overall health of natural ecosystems, and keep Alaska's moose and caribou populations healthy and strong."

For more information on the plight of wolves, check out the following website: www.care2.com

Significance: Families, whether blood or extended, form the basis of society. Red wolf's message is that we need to honor family units regardless of whether they are traditional—as in mom, dad, and children—or nontraditional, as in households with gay parents. Tolerance for nontraditional families should be increased through education and the passage of laws that allow nontraditional couples the same rights as traditional couples.

ENDANGERED BIRDS

California Condor

Condors are the largest flying birds in North America. Millennia ago, they lived on both coasts of North America, from British Columbia to Baja California, and from New York to Florida. By around 1900, the population count plunged and the bird's existence was limited to California.

In 1982, there were fewer than twenty condors remaining in the wild. Today, there are around two hundred. Part of the reason the increase hasn't been greater is that condors breed only once every two years and produce just one egg. These birds are monogamous and mate for life. Both parents take turns incubating the egg and feeding the baby until it learns to find its own food.

These birds are inquisitive, playful, and communicate with hisses, growls, grunts, and body language. The condor's wings can span more than nine feet from tip to tip and instead of flapping them to stay aloft, they ride the wind currents. They're scavengers, but tend to watch for other scavengers who are feeding rather than relying on their sense of smell.

Significance: In a planetary sense, we are unable to adequately deal with all the waste we produce as a species. From ordinary garbage and sewage to nuclear wastes, we're inundated by the refuse of civilization. On a personal level, we lack the bigger picture—the "bird's eye view."

Crow

There are currently twelve species of crow that are endangered. The Hawaiian crow was so critically endangered that in 1993, there were only thirteen of the birds remaining in a small area in Hawaii. Crows are generally black—a sleek, shiny ebony black—but Australian magpies, which are in the same family, are bright red and green.

Both parents build the nest, but only the mother incubates the eggs. While she incubates, the male crow hunts for food and feeds her. In some species of crow, the breeding pair establish a territory with their partner and remain in that area as long as both partners are alive. But in other species, crows live in social groups that consist of the young from the previous year, who stick around to help with the new youngsters.

When you consider that there are over a hundred species of crows and jays, these birds adapt fairly well to urban environments, where they forage on almost anything. But in areas like Hawaii, where land is limited and habitats vanish through overdevelopment, it's a different story altogether.

Significance: In a broad sense, all birds are messengers. But the crow, like its brother the raven, is often associated with messages between the living and the dead, with birth and rebirth, and with shamanistic magic. The endangered status of this bird symbolizes our collective need to embrace the magical in everyday life. On a personal level, Crow may be telling us that we need to be more open to reincarnation and the possibility that we share past-life connections with many of our loved ones.

Parrots

Not all parrots are endangered. But all of them, more than seventy species, are threatened or at risk, and the wild-bird trade is at fault. Worldwide, there seems to be an insatiable hunger to own wild birds, and parrots are the most popular of all cage birds. And this hunger is nothing new. Ancient Egyptians had a fondness for rose-ringed parakeets.

The current list for endangered parrots is downright depressing— seventy-one species that include the lorikeet, the salmon-crested cockatoo, the orange-bellied parrot, the night parrot, and the macaw. The largest parrot, the hyacinth macaw of South America, is at critically low numbers. It's doubtful whether it will even survive in the wild.

Brazil and Indonesia are notoriously oblivious to conservation. These two countries alone account for more than twenty-five percent of all threatened bird species.

Some parrots, like macaws, probably mate for life. Other parrot pairs join family flocks. In South Florida, flocks of wild green parrots often take to the skies in the evening, squawking and making quite a racket. Many of them were once pets that escaped. In Fort Lauderdale, a flock of wild green parrots that grace the evening skies are believed to be descendants of parrots that escaped a carnival act some years ago.

Parrots are extremely vocal, terrific mimics, and are capable of speech. If you have any doubt at all about their intelligence, read *The Parrot Who Owned Me,* by Joanna Burger. You'll never think of parrots in quite the same light again!

With the proliferation of shows like those on *Animal Planet* and the publication of books like *The Parrot Who Owned Me* and *The Parrot's Lament,* public awareness about all animals is raised. But will it be enough to prevent the extinction of the parrot?

Significance: On both a global and a personal level, the message of Parrot is about communication. We must learn to communicate honestly with people whose cultures and beliefs are vastly different from our own and use diplomacy rather than force to bring about change.

Peregrine Falcons

This bird was removed from the endangered list in August, 1999. But we're including it here because its population remains under scrutiny and because pesticides nearly wiped them out.

DDT brought these birds to the brink of extinction. When the peregrine falcon ate birds that had ingested seeds soaked in pesticide, the falcon either stopped laying eggs or laid eggs with extremely thin shells. When the birds tried to incubate these thin-shelled eggs, the shells broke. When DDT was banned, the falcon population began to rise again.

Like a number of birds on the endangered species list, peregrines mate for life and return to the same nesting site every year. The male and female share the incubation of the eggs, which must be turned, a process that the birds accomplish with their feet or their beaks. The incubation period is around thirty-three days.

Peregrines fly extremely fast, particularly in their downward dives, where their speeds can reach speeds in excess of a hundred miles an hour. Most of their prey are other birds, which are caught in midair. They apparently don't like flying too close to the ground and usually don't fly below the level of their nest, even if their prey falls to the ground. Not surprisingly, they have great eyesight.

Significance: On a global level, the fact that the falcon was taken off the endangered list is encouraging. It indicates a growing awareness collectively and individually that everything and everyone on the planet is inter-connected. However, these birds were removed from the endangered list before the 2000 election. The Bush administration has shown its in-difference to environmental issues by its refusal to sign the Kyoto treaty and by placing the interests of big business (read: profit, greed) over those of the environment. This is a species to watch.

Whooping Crane

These beautiful birds were once found throughout much of central and western North America. The breeding populations covered an area from central Illinois northwestward to the Arctic coast in the MacKenzie River area. The birds then wintered along the coast of the Gulf of Mexico from Florida to central Mexico. That's a pretty wide area. Yet, their numbers were never huge.

By the late eighteenth century, their numbers had fallen to about 1500 birds and by 1941, only 21 whooping cranes were left. Fifteen of these birds migrated to an unknown breeding area in northern Canada, and six birds stayed in Louisiana year-round. Since 1938, conservation efforts have brought about a slow increase in the whooping crane population.

The birds were listed under the Endangered Species Act in 1973, and there are several recovery programs in place. Operation Migration, the International Crane Foundation, and a team from the Patuxent Wildlife Research Center in Laurel, Maryland, currently run one such project. In mid-October 2003, fifteen young whooping cranes took flight for the third year in a row, for a 1,200 mile journey from Wisconsin to wintering grounds in Florida. The birds flew for twenty-three miles behind an ultralight aircraft before they reached their first stopover in central Wisconsin. This incredible feat was beautifully told in the movie *Fly Away Home,* but with geese rather than cranes.

Biologists will monitor the cranes throughout the winter and track them next spring when they return to Wisconsin unaided.

Whooping cranes mate for life, but if the mate dies, they sometimes accept a new one. They return every year to the same nesting area, and both parents are involved in incubating the eggs.

Significance: The continued endangerment of the whooping crane may point to the fissures within the family structure—our individual families and the family of man.

ENDANGERED REPTILES AND AMPHIBIANS

~~~~~~~~~~~~~~~~~~~~~~~~~~~~~~~~~

Crocodiles

Never forget that reptiles once ruled the earth. In fact, if you need to be reminded, rent *Jurassic Park* or, better yet, head out to a zoo or a natural habitat where you can see an alligator or a crocodile in the flesh.

A variety of crocodiles are endangered and for a number of reasons: Hunting for the skin trade, sports shooting, malicious persecution, and habitat loss. On the North American continent, the American crocodile is endangered.

This strange animal looks like it escaped from a movie set. It's shockingly primal. In the upper jaw on each side is a notch where the fourth tooth in the lower jaw fits. Even when the mouth is shut, the tooth is visible, so that crocodiles always seem to have a mocking smirk on their faces.

Crocodiles deal with extreme environments and nature has designed them to survive well in such extremes. They absorb excessive amounts of salt through their skins and while eating and they can't excrete it unless they drink large amounts of fresh water, which flushes the salt through their kidneys. It's a catch-22. If you live in a saline environment, there isn't much fresh water to be had. So nature designed salt glands on their tongues and in their tear ducts that allow them to excrete excess salt without losing valuable water.

Both crocodiles and alligators are attentive mothers. They lay dozens of eggs in mounds that are scraped up soil and vegetation and don't hesitate to defend their tests from poachers and intruders. Sometimes, the father also remains in the area to help defend the nest. The eggs incubate for sixty to a hundred days, then the young crocs start making sounds inside the eggs. The mother then digs a hole in the mound to release the babies and carries them gently in her mouth to the water.

The temperature in which the eggs are incubated is vital for the survival of the eggs, but also determines the gender. Temperatures less than 88 degrees produce females and temperatures higher than 90 degrees produce males. Temperatures in between produce a mix of males and females.

The crocodile, slow-moving on land, can propel itself out of the water in an explosive, violent fashion, one of its most effective skills as a predator.

The American crocodile is found primarily in South Florida, in the mangrove swamps that are diminishing at startling rates due to overbuilding. Their current population is estimated at between 400 and 1000.

Significance: The endangered status of the American crocodile symbolizes Western man's inability to adapt to extremes. In a personal sense, it represents our need to take each day as it comes, to go with the flow.

Sea Turtles

Sometime during the age of dinosaurs, the giant land tortoises returned to the sea and became sea turtles, marine reptiles that have managed to survive until modern times. But just barely. The loggerhead sea turtle, the green sea turtle, and the leatherback sea turtle nest on the beaches of South Florida from April to September every year. The loggerhead is the most common to these nesting grounds.

Even though sea turtles enjoy a double protection—from the Endangered Species Act as well as Florida statues, their populations have been reduced through development of coastal areas and the capture of adult turtles for eggs, meat, leather, and tortoise shells. The Kemp's Ridley, another species of sea turtle, has been brought to the doorstep of extinction through incidental capture in fishing nets and shrimp trawls.

The nesting behavior of sea turtles is fascinating to observe. During the summer in South Florida, people line up on beaches at night to watch loggerheads make their nests. The female crawls out of the water and up the beach to a point above the high tide line. With her rear flippers, she digs a hole about eighteen inches deep, then begins to fill it with a hundred or more eggs the size of golf balls. Once she has laid all her eggs, she covers the hole with sand and spreads sand around the area so the exact location of the eggs can't be detected easily. Then she leaves, never to see her hatchlings or that nesting site again.

In South Florida, the nests are sometimes moved to a safer area of the beach and then protected by wire mesh fences that mark their location. Due to the many houses, people, and lights along the South Florida beaches, the safer areas are usually well away from lights, which can disorient the hatchlings and cause them to turn away from the water.

After fifty to fifty-five days, the eggs hatch and the little turtles begin a dangerous journey toward adulthood. It's impossible to know how many hatchlings survive. The most optimistic guess is that one in a thousand makes it to adulthood; the most pessimistic estimate is one in ten thousand.

Significance: Our children are our future. Sea Turtle's message is that we need to improve child protection laws, to correct serious flaws in the child welfare system, and create greater understanding through education about the perils of youth—drugs, gangs, teenage pregnancies, and indifferent parents.

OTHER ENDANGERED AND THREATENED ANIMALS

We've listed a variety of other endangered or threatened animals. Test your intuition to come up with the significance for each animal on the list. You may want to go through the list once and jot down whatever comes to mind, then do a little research on the animal's behaviors and life cycle and its role in mythology and folklore.

African Wild Dog

Aye-Aye

Bald Eagle

Basking Shark

Bengal Tiger

Boa Constrictor

Brown Pelican

Cheetah

Chimpanzee

Gazelle

Gorilla

Gray Wolf

Great Egret

Humpback Whale

Penguins

Koala

Lynx

Otter

Panda

Panther

Puma

Siberian Tiger

Snow Leopard

Viceroy Butterfly

White Rhinoceros

Yak

Zebra

PREDICTIONS

~~~~~~~~~~~~~~~~~~

We selected a handful of endangered animals and Trish asked Millie to give her predictions on each animal's future and what that meant for us as a species. Here are the results.

Blue Whale

"The whale population could fall as low as 9,000, but they will recover. We need more legislation to save them."

With the current administration's lack of concern about the environment, Trish asked Millie if Bush would be re-elected in 2004. "I don't know who's going to win," she replied. "But honey, you and I will be happy about the election." The only way either of us would be happy about the election is if Bush isn't re-elected.

Crocodile

"He's tough. But he'll last forever. He'll find a place to hide, just as we will."

Crow

"Crow, like the eagle, will fly to the highest mountaintop to project itself and its species. Studying Crow will make us, as a society, less afraid of death."

Florida Panther

"We're crowding him out of his natural habitat and it's going to get worse for him. Because of this overcrowding, our food supply (man's) could be in danger. It won't happen overnight, but it *will* happen. Mountains would be safer for the Florida panther."

Giant Panda

"As we destroy forested areas, the already endangered panda may not survive. The real reason they're still on the planet is because people pay money to see them. As a result, we as people are becoming cold, indifferent, and losing our softer, more sensitive sides."

Gorilla

"To me, the endangered gorilla speaks of fear. We're fearful of other people and other countries and we're quick to destroy them in the hope that it will make us safer. I feel there won't be many of these creatures left."

Grizzly Bear

"He'll be driven farther and farther away from us—and for us, collectively, it means we're losing power."

Manatee

"They stand for our elderly. I feel tears when I think of them (the elderly). They've been used and abused, just as the manatees have been. Unless we learn more compassion for the elderly, we'll become a throwaway society. The prognosis for the manatee is good. They'll rebound and will be able to reproduce more often. This means that overall, things will improve for the elderly as well."

Monarch Butterfly

"They'll survive. And so will we, but not before we destroy much of the planet's natural beauty."

Penguin

"By virtue of where they live, they'll survive. Even if the polar ice caps continue to melt, Penguin will persevere."

Sea Turtle

"We're polluting the oceans, which destroys not only the sea turtle but other species of fish. As a people, this endangered animal symbolizes that our freedom to come and go as we please may be at risk."

Whooping Crane

"This crane would be safer farther north. It represents that the family structure will have to build itself up again, just as Crane has done. As things worsen in the world, the family will become a more tightly knit structure."

Wild Mustang

"To me, the endangered status of this magnificent creature means that we're in danger of losing our civil liberties—our freedoms—as government intrudes more and more into our lives."

Wolf (Red and Gray)

"I see the Red Wolf being okay in the east, but not in the West. People still believe Wolf is a killer, yet they take this descendant, the dog, into their homes. They aren't willing to have compassion for the Wolf. The Gray Wolf goes farther north and finds ways of protecting itself. For us, I feel we must become more tolerant of different lifestyles whether we agree with them or not. We have to learn that love is love."

15

Putting It All Together

~~~~~~

While we were working on *Animal Totems,* we had a cluster of animal experiences that illustrate what this book is all about. We want to share these stories so that you can see how we interpreted these experiences in light of our daily lives and what was going on at the time.

On a Friday night, Trish and her husband, Rob, had left to pick up their daughter, Megan. When the three of them got back to the house, Millie greeted them at the door with a very tiny, hairless creature that she was holding in a napkin.

"I kept hearing squeaking," she said. "And two of your cats were acting strangely. I found the little guy in the middle of the kitchen floor. I think it's a mouse."

The mouse looked newly born—not only was it bald, but the eyes were still shut, the ears weren't visible. Our biggest concern was where the mice had come from. All three of the cats had been in the house, so that meant there had to be a nest inside. We looked everywhere, but the only thing we found was another tiny, bald mouse. We put them both in a towel and since it was hot outside, put them on a table outside, where nothing (like cats) could get them.

That night, Trish's oldest cat, Whiskers, got violently ill and seemed to be having a hard time breathing. The next morning, we took him—and the two mice—to the vet. We suspected that he had eaten the mother, although we never found any entrails or blood to suggest that. The vet treated him with anti-vomiting medicine and an antibiotic. She thought it was likely that he'd eaten the mother and that the change in food had upset his digestive system. She also confirmed that the hairless critters were mice and instructed Megan in how to take care of them.

Mice symbolize details and since it was Millie who found the first mouse, we figured that she needed to pay closer attention to details concerning the book. However, the mice were found in the MacGregor kitchen—sustenance?—and in the family room, which we felt represented all of us to one degree or another.

When we got home, Rob said that two turkey vultures had been sitting at the end of the driveway and that Jessie, the golden retriever, had chased them off. Vultures, considering what they eat, have unusual digestive systems, so there was a parallel to Whisker's problem. Vultures are also associated with death and rebirth and that made us wonder if Whiskers was going to pass over or if one of the mice was the reincarnation of Megan's pet mouse, which had died a month ago. The fact that Jessie chased off the vultures seemed telling, too. As a dog, she symbolizes loyalty and devotion and by chasing off the intruding vultures, she was displaying her loyalty to the family.

Megan, a double Virgo, a sign known for its attention to details, made the hairless guys a bed in a small box with a heating pad in it. She fed them every hour or two over the next twenty-four hours. We went back to work on the book, shifting the material around and paying much closer attention to the details the mice seemed to be addressing.

One of the mice died within the first day, the second mouse died the following night. Whiskers improved over the next two days and was back to normal by the third day.

This story perfectly illustrates the way animals and synchronicity often work in our daily lives. The events were a faithful reflection of what was going on and prompted us to rethink how we were approaching this book.

THE ONE-LEGGED OWL

Several years ago, Trish's mother was in an Alzheimer's unit and her father was living with her family. One Sunday afternoon, Megan and her friend came racing into the kitchen, telling Trish to hurry up and look at something. There was an owl perched on the atrium fence outside Trish's father's bedroom. Trish knew that owls, as messengers, sometimes portended death and was immediately concerned that it meant her father, who had Parkinson's, was going to die soon. Then she noticed that the owl was perched on just one leg and she and Megan and her friend hurried outside to get a closer look at it.

The bird was a burrowing owl, an endangered species that lives in ground burrows and is usually active at dusk. At the time this happened, it was noon, so the time of day was unusual. The owl was from a family of burrowing owls that had nested in the backyard of a neighboring house, and it wasn't the least bit startled as Trish and the two girls approached it. They were able to get within a few feet and saw that the owl wasn't just perched on one leg; part of its left leg was missing.

Unsettled by the event, Trish convinced herself it didn't mean anything. But at nine the next morning, the phone rang. It was the Alzheimer's facility. Her mother was on her way to the emergency room, presumably for a broken hip. But by the end of the day, the prognosis was even worse than a broken hip. Her mother's left hipbone—the same leg that was partially missing on the owl—had disintegrated completely and she wasn't a candidate for hip replacement surgery because she didn't have the presence of mind necessary for the rehab.

"So what are the alternatives?" Trish asked.

"Oh," the doctor said casually, "we do wonderful things with pain management nowadays."

It was easy for him to say. It wasn't his mother.

Her mother went into a nursing home and for the last three weeks of her life was on such heavy doses of morphine that she was rarely conscious.

In the end, the owl knew weeks ahead of time—and delivered the message.

THE CROW AND THE CAT

Pauline, a friend of Millie's, saw a crow landing in her yard, next to her adult son. She screamed for him to shoo the crow away, but he didn't believe his mother's warning that the crow was a harbinger of bad news. Immediately after Pauline's warning, a black cat strolled up close to the crow. Again, Pauline warned her son of the black cat bringing bad luck to them. He laughed and picked up the cat.

Her son put the cat on the ground and headed for the house and up the steep stairs that led into it. She heard him remark that the steps seemed steeper and he felt that one day he would fall down those steps and accidentally kill himself. The following day, as he was going up the steps, he fell backwards upon the cement and was instantly killed.

This is another instance where a messenger—the crow—delivered a warning. But in this instance, the warning was backed up by a black cat.

We would love to hear your stories about animal encounters. Please contact us at www.booktalk.com/t.j.macgregor

PART THREE

ANIMALS AT A GLANCE

"My animal companions are part of my family."

—Megan MacGregor, age 14

"Many of us seem to have lost all sense of restraint toward animals, an understanding of natural boundaries, a respect for them as being with needs and wants and a place and purpose of their own."

—From *Dominion: The Power of Man, the Suffering of Animals, and a Call to Mercy,* by Matthew Scully

Alphabetical Listing of Animals

A

〰〰〰〰〰〰〰〰

Aardvark
When one of these "living fossils" appears in your life, it's time to explore your personal mythology. Where do you fit in the grander scheme of things?

Albatross
Are you feeling unappreciated? Do you feel like running? Don't mind asking for help to boost you into flight to a better feeling. You mate for life.

Alligator
Survivor. Adaptability. Be patient, bide your time, keep your own counsel. When you spot an opportunity, act with swiftness and determination. Act on your intuition.

American Goldfinch
You are gregarious and are one who enjoys your mate and family groups—picnics, reunions, weddings, and so on. You're the family dancer and singer and should attend all those functions because your presence brings other people joy.

American Woodcock
You don't like to be in the forefront of things. It is almost as though you camouflage yourself so you can't be seen. Don't hide. You have much to offer the world.

〰〰〰〰〰〰〰〰〰〰〰〰〰〰〰〰〰〰〰〰〰〰〰〰〰〰

Anhinga

You easily get bogged down in the stuff of daily life. It's necessary to be in the sun to revitalize your energy.

Ant

Are you a workaholic? Are you putting in long hours working for others? Nurture your own dreams.

Anteater

So you have a Jimmy Durante nose! No need to get a complex about it. There's always the plastic surgeon. However, when Anteater shows up in your life, there may be a liar close by. Remember Pinocchio?

Antelope

You're going to encounter someone who is graceful and nice-looking. This person could become a romantic partner. Rapid advancement is guaranteed.

Armadillo

Your armor protects you. You delve deeply to ferret out the truth. It may be necessary to set up boundaries between yourself and others. Like "Mike Hammer," you can go with the flow.

B

Baboon

If you're male, you're often cantankerous, causing confusion with your barking and blustering in an attempt to intimidate others. The female and little ones must pay attention to you. Cool it, friend! Being called a baboon is hardly flattering.

Badger

Keep after it. Don't quit. Don't take no for an answer. Whatever you're doing needs doing. As the Dalai Lama says, "Never give up!" Badger symbolizes aggressiveness, passion and drive.

Bat

Intuitive awareness. Past-life connections. Luck. A change in sleeping habits. You need a change in perspective.

Bear

Associated with personal power. Don't hide or hibernate all year round. Bring what you love out into the open and apply it to the world in which you live. Self-knowledge is vital now.

Grizzly Bear

Relates to parenting, particularly for a mother. You fiercely guard your children. Both male and female strongly defend their breeding territory. Approximately 850 bears exist in the lower 48 states. (Threatened species)

Beaver

Hard work and constructive efforts get you where you want to go. Just keep at it. You'll get there.

Bee

Sincere, hard work, a team effort. Represents a mutual endeavor in which all parties must serve one another if everyone is to prosper. In folklore, there's a belief that when a beekeeper or the person who tended to the bees passed away, it was important to "tell the bees." This belief probably came about because bees are associated with pollination and life. Communicate clearly and concisely.

Honeybee: Generosity. Sweetness. Team work. (Endangered)

Bumble Bee: Service, communication and healing. Are you communicating with those around you? When you start communicating you can be of service and may start a healing of which you are not aware. (Endangered)

Considerable folklore surrounds the stinging of bees to cure a number of ailments, including arthritis. Millie had a personal experience with this sort of healing. She had been having a severe problem with her thumb and one day, while sitting on her front porch, a large bumble bee touched down on the base of it and stung her severely. It left its stinger and flew away. Although there was initial pain, shortly afterwards the thumb began to heal and quit hurting.

Beetle

You may need to protect yourself now from barbs and criticism. You'll get through this period by keeping your own counsel and maintaining a low profile.

Black Widow Spider

Patience. Don't be afraid to let your creativity shine. Be innovative, quick when the situation calls for it, and coy when you have to be coy. If you're male, be cautious around your partner!

Blue Bird

You will soon be very happy and contentment will reign about you. This bird with the golden voice indicates freedom from problems and apprehension.

Blue Wildebeest

Loosen up, chill out, have some fun. You're gregarious, a favorite at parties, but perhaps you've forgotten how to enjoy yourself. (Endangered)

Boa Constrictor

Is something squeezing you into a bad position? Being adaptable and adept at most situations, you can use your senses to locate the problem and get rid of it quickly.

Boar

Don't be a martyr. You have the courage to ward off problems and potential disaster. Strength and fearlessness are your greatest assets. Financially, things are about to improve.

Buffalo (bison)

Your focus now should be on spiritual communication and your spiritual beliefs. Since this animal is endangered, we, as a nation, are in danger of losing our abundance. With a deficit now soaring into the trillions, nearly four million jobs lost since the presidential election in 2000, and economic policies that seem to favor only the wealthy, some would say our economy is in trouble. Buffalo is also associated with feminine energy. Is it time to soften up your perspective on life? To draw on your own gentleness? (Endangered)

Butterfly

Resurrection, fertility, transformation, spirits of the dead. Expect profound changes in your relationships, finances, and your personal power.

Buzzard

What do you need to clean up in your life? Keep at the problem until you find the solution. It's time to recycle old ideas.

(

Canary

The news you hear may be unpleasant. Don't judge the bird by its beautiful plumage! Live in the moment. Let music soothe your soul. You may need to listen to your own music, your own drummer. Bird of warning. Miners took canaries down in the shafts as an early warning system against the dangers of gas in the air. If the canary died, the men fled back to the surface. After 9/11, the sale of canaries in Manhattan rose dramatically, as people rushed to pet stores to buy the bird that would immediately tell them if the city was under chemical attack.

In gangster parlance, a "canary" sings to betray his friends to the cops. Either way, that bright and pretty bird has come to symbolize bad news.

Cardinal

You're a fierce defender of your territory and can be very aggressive. If you're not involved, then romance is forthcoming and you'll bond well with your mate. Cardinal's appearance indicates that joy through beauty and music is on its way.

Cat (domestic)

You need more independence in your personal relationships. Give loyalty where it's due. Try changing your sleeping habits to increase your creativity.

Ancient Rome considered the cat as a symbol of liberty and any representation of liberty had a cat reposing at her feet. (Since cats are so opposed to restraint, the "liberty" tag fits.) No animal is so opposed to restraint as a cat, therefore "liberty." Ancient Egypt held the cat as sacred. Killing a cat at that time (even by accident) was punishable by death. The wildcat was once considered a hunter god in American myths, and was thought to be the younger brother of the coyote. The cat (along with the snake) is under a curse in Buddhism, as they were the only two creatures who did not weep at the death of Buddha.

Caterpillar

Don't worry about your looks or about appearances. Beauty lies within. You're about to undergo a transformation of some kind that will allow your inner beauty to show.

Centipede

When frightened or worried, you become introverted and run and hide. Fight your fears. Although you're usually a gentle soul, you tend to get emotionally stressed out. You may be running at full speed in your life. Slow down so you can listen and heed your own advice.

Chameleon

Adaptability and camouflage. Chameleon's appearance may relate to your sexuality. It can be warning you that you should blend in rather than draw attention to yourself.

Chamois

You're nimble and show endurance. You're sometimes audacious, but can survive in nearly any situation. Your strength lies in the group.

Cheetah

You're in danger of backing off from a challenge. Don't do it. You can beat out the competition. You think fast on your feet, and your mind moves swiftly. Once you rise to the challenge, expect growth and quick progress. (Endangered)

Chicken

You proclaim the area that belongs to you and yours. If you're a woman, then be careful—your children may not be perfect and may need correcting instead of defending.

Chiggers

That itch you feel is real. Don't hide. You're in need of some rest and recreation!

Chimney Swift

A good career field would be anything to do with travel. You may be taking a trip. You're able to adapt to change now, so don't resist opportunities that come your way.

Chipmunk

Guard your resources, keep your own counsel. Listen, don't speak. Trust what you hear in the other person's voice. Stash some money away, replenish your reserves.

Cockroach

Be more persistent. Follow your instincts. You're known by the company you keep!

Condor

You need the bird's eye view now. It's possible that people you knew years ago are now "recycling" through your life again.

Coot

"Crazy as a Coot" often applies to your actions because of your awkward and ridiculous ways of trying to be funny. However, you may be able to turn this ability into income!

Cougar

You need solitude to work out your challenges. Find out what you want and pursue it. You should investigate alternative therapies.

Cow (bull)

If you're trying to get pregnant, the cow and the bull are excellent symbols. Together, these two animals represent yin and yang, the moon and the sun, male and female. The bull brought nourishment through slaughtering and so became known as the animal symbolizing fertility through sacrifice.

In India, the cow is a sacred animal not to be killed. In Celtic mythology, the cow appears as a provider of perpetual nourishment. Cattle were highly regarded by Celts as the most important animal for their sustenance and welfare and the basis for wealth and prestige. During medieval times, the superstition arose that cattle would kneel at the stroke of midnight on Christmas eve.

There are many English and Welsh tales of fairy cows who gave never-ending milk until their generosity was abused by some greedy human, causing the loss of the cow or her powers. Cattle diseases were often attributed to fairies, elves, or witches.

As recently as the nineteenth century, some farmers would sacrifice one healthy calf or cow as a symbolic offering so that the herd might be spared from cattle plague. Bull worship was practiced in Egypt and Greece. In Roman and Greek mythology, there are seven legends of the bull—the Minotaur is the most familiar. The bull is said to provide insight into past lives and, of course, is associated with the astrological sign of Taurus. It's to your benefit to read about the sign of Taurus when Bull or Cow appear in your life.

Coyote

The trickster. Be careful about whom you trust. Who are you trying to fool? You're confronted with a tough choice—the answer may lie in your spiritual beliefs and practice. You're looking for devotion from a partner or commitment on an issue.

Crab

Are you moody? Inclined to addictions? You may encounter a situation where you're going to be cornered, and you will have to fight for what you believe. Your home truly is your castle, and when Crab appears, issues surrounding your home and your mother may surface. You're talented, but find it difficult to get to the top because of your attitude. The crab is the animal associated with the astrological sign of Cancer. It would be to your benefit to read about this sign.

Crane

Be vigilant. Practice patience. Look over your shoulder. Know who your friends are and know exactly where you are. In mythology, the crane is often the messenger of the gods and was thought to have great intelligence and vigilance. There may be an element of spirituality in your experience with Crane. Here's one man's story about an experience with a crane:

Jim had been having a lot of bad luck. His finances were lost, his daughter eloped, and his wife left him. He had become somber and started drinking until it was becoming an issue. One afternoon he noticed something strange on his mountain pond. A crane was sitting there; this was not a usual area for a crane as they are normally not seen in the mountains.

As the crane kept hanging around, things in Jim's life began to shift. Friends began to visit him and he not longer felt the need to visit the local bar. He called his daughter to ask her to forgive him for being so stubborn about her elopement. Over a period of time he and his wife started talking by phone and they decided to renew their marriage vows. This did not happen overnight. The crane stayed by the pond for three years.

When Jim, his wife, daughter, and son-in-law became a family again, the crane disappeared.

Cricket

Luck. Communication. If the cricket is found inside your home, expect luck and serendipity in some area of your life. Cricket also brings heightened intuition and the importance and power of your beliefs in shaping your reality. Communicate clearly about what you believe.

Crocodile

You have great parenting skills and would do well with many children around you—either as a parent or in teaching or in coaching sports. New knowledge to add to your old knowledge and skills will be forthcoming. (Endangered)

Crow

You may be in a dangerous situation or an unhealthy relationship. Listen to your own intuition and heed the advice of those close to you. Crow is a messenger and sometimes appears to announce death—not yours, but the death of someone you know.

Cuckoo

These birds are renowned for their songs. When Cuckoo appears, it's likely that you will have reason to sing and to celebrate. Change is on the way.

D

Deer

You'll be required to adapt to a situation or within a relationship. You may have to blend in to succeed. Your spiritual beliefs may be in flux, but that's fine because your beliefs come from a place of gentleness and peace.

Dodo

Innocent and friendly, you are often gullible. Be aware that others are not as sweet and friendly as you. Keep your eyes open to what is happening around you and keep yourself protected. (Extinct)

Dog

Loyalty and unconditional love. The appearance of a dog in your life indicates a deepening of loyalty, love, and commitment between you and the people you care for. It may also be telling you that you need to open your heart.

Dolphin

Live in the moment and relish it for all that it's worth. Allow the intuitive and spiritual dimensions of your life to shine through. You're here for a purpose. Your sex life is about to heat up, possibly with someone you have known in previous lives.

Donkey

You're a workaholic and may need to lighten your load and de-stress. Consider delegating responsibility to others.

Dove

You're looking for no one less than your soulmate. You value loyalty, family, and mutual love and respect. Some issue connected to a relationship will be resolved within a month.

Dragonfly

You receive the news for which you have been waiting. And it's good!

Duck

Quack with laughter, shake your troubles off, and waddle away from it all. Sometimes you're a real cutie and everybody loves you.

E

Eagle

You're a crowd pleaser. Your intuition and clairvoyance are heightened now. Unlike the hawk who perches alone, eagles will congregate in big groups, especially if there's a fish canning factory nearby! For all their apparent dignity, they're not above taking hand-outs, and in some locales they are quite the pest. The embarrassing truth is that the eagle symbolizes someone who has a better reputation than he probably deserves.

In the early sixties, there were only four hundred breeding pairs of bald eagles left in the U.S. Author Rachel Carson, in her masterpiece *Silent Spring,* wrote: "The trend...may well make it necessary for us to find a new national emblem." However, with the passage of the Endangered Species Act and the banning of DDT, bald eagles were moved from the endangered list to the threatened list in 1995. Today, there are more than 6,000 breeding pairs.

Earthworm

You're necessary to the people in your private world. Cheer up. You can restore your life when things go wrong, but it may require you to give up or surrender attitudes, situations, and relationships that no longer work. Solitude and meditation would benefit you now.

Eel

Mysterious, intuitive, unusual sexuality, "electric" experiences. You may be surprised by a quick shock, but it won't kill you. To avoid being shocked again, keep your eyes open to what's going on around you. Watch out for people who may be charismatic, but slippery.

Egret

You join a group of people who share a particular interest or passion. Travel may be involved, but it's related to business.

Elephant

Elephant augurs well for increased good health and the loyalty of friends and family. (Endangered)

Emu

Your curiosity may get you in trouble. The issue here is single parenting if you're a man and indifference to your children if you're a woman.

F

Falcon (Kestral)

Know when to proceed and commit yourself to action if you wish to be successful. Study the "lay of the land" before going ahead.

Fish

A fish swimming up to you in your dreams indicates change and communication. Accept these changes in your home with unselfishness.

Flamingo

If you worry about looking awkward or strange, "look again." You are quite beautiful and graceful. Try to build your confidence through a cosmetology or modeling class. Get out and exercise. In yoga, there's a posture called the crane (or the stork). You may want to do that posture, and others, to increase your balance and flexibility.

Fox

Family concerns are heightened when Fox appears. It's part of the ongoing process to create a new beginning.

Finch (Zebra)

Your gregarious nature leads you to be involved with large groups of people. Those people may gather at your favorite "watering hole." You're easy to approach because of your friendliness. Be careful of imbibing too much or your next gathering place could possibly be AA.

Firefly

Few creatures are greeted by more love and delight, and yet children tear off their glowing tails to make "rings," or imprison them in jars. Like the firefly, be quick in order to be safe. Shine your light, then don't hang around. You're searching for a mate. Keep showing your light; it will lead you to find the love of your life.

Flea

Quit jumping around and being a childish annoyance to those around you. Or perhaps there's someone in your life who is annoying you. Identify the itch.

Fly

Omnivorous. Multifaceted vision. Clinging. Maybe something would stop pestering you if you could look at it from a different perspective. Someone is about to land on you and suck out your life blood or knowledge. You need to change the way you see things. Develop flexibility.

Frog

Don't judge the frog prince in your life by his looks. The love of your life may be right in front of you. A transformative event is closer than you think. New experiences in your personal and business life will arrive soon.

G

Gecko

You have a gift for communication. To improve your skills, join a speech help group such as "Toastmasters International." You'll be surprised at your hidden capabilities.

Gnat

Watch your eyes! It's time for those new glasses or contact lenses or surgery to take care of those cataracts. You may be very susceptible to "pink eye," or conjunctivitis.

Goat

You set goals and push against any obstacle to attain them. Be diligent and tenacious and you'll succeed. Don't become discouraged; you'll get to where you want to go. Associated with the zodiac sign of Capricorn.

Nanny Goat: The goat was often used as a sacrifice by poorer people who could not afford a bull or an ox in religious ceremonies. This little animal is tenacious and a diligent worker. Don't sacrifice yourself and your family to your job or work. Being a workaholic isn't always rewarded financially, or even with appreciation.

Golden Mole

If you think you made a big boo-boo, don't worry. You do more good than not and others are accepting of you.

Goldfish

Abundance and prosperity are coming into your life quite soon. There's an element of spiritual protection connected to Goldfish.

Goose

A perfectionist, you wish to soar to the top and lead the formation. You're very versatile, but take note that everything and everybody is not perfect. You too are not perfect and need not be so judgmental. Your home is extremely important to you now and if you're traveling, you return there safely.

Gorilla

This huge, scary animal is really the kind one of the ape family. His appearance in your dreams indicates that you have strength and endurance. If Gorilla appears, it's time to rent *Gorillas in the Mist*, about Diane Fossey's valiant attempt to save gorillas in Africa.

Millie dreamed she was in a pool of clear green water. In the water was a small green snake, a beaver, and on the side of the pool was a large gray wolf with piercing eyes. Coming toward the water was a gorilla. None of these animals frightened her. She was open to the spirit of these animals and knew their meaning. The snake was bringing wisdom. The beaver showed that she was busy as a beaver. The wolf was her teacher and the gorilla indicated she would have the strength to handle all the things she was doing. The clear green water indicated her growth spiritually.

Grasshopper

Ravenous. A threat to the harvest. Seeing a single grasshopper may be a sign of a problem having to do with a "harvest" that needs handling right now. Seeing many grasshoppers may be a warning not to jeopardize your success by letting problems build up until they're overwhelming. Or, it could just mean, who's eating everything in sight?

Groundhog

You gnaw away at your problems and store up "goodies" for the winter. It's important to be alert to new challenges that will soon be facing you. Dismiss your fears of poverty. You will never be the "man on the street" or a "bag lady." Here's a story about one woman's experience with a groundhog.

The neighborhood gardens were being ravaged by a groundhog who had burrowed in a nearby field. Each gardener attempted to find ways of ridding themselves of this little pest. Shooting the animal wasn't an option because it was against the law to use firearms in town. A trap was tried, but this frisky fellow with the sharp teeth gnawed his way through the heavy wire trap.

Sensing this animal's need to eat brought Millie to the door one morning. She could see that the groundhog was in her garden chewing away on her tomatoes. Millie spoke to him and told him if he would no longer invade her garden, she would provide him with food every evening.

Millie stuck to her end of the bargain and Grady, as she'd named the groundhog, no longer came into her garden. The neighbors didn't have a clue why Grady continued to raid their property and asked Millie about her secret. When she revealed it, the idea of talking to an animal was met with disdain. By fall, Millie was the only one who had a garden that had not been decimated by Grady and his family.

Grouse

You're more likely to be heard than seen and that's okay for right now. But make sure your territory is well-known and that you can shock and confuse your adversary when need be.

Guinea fowl (Hen)

Don't fear what is ahead. You can squawk and are capable of defending yourself by kicking out against your attackers. Guineas are also known to be great "watchdogs" and make tremendous noise when strangers appear near or upon their home ground, so be assured that others are also looking out for you.

Gull

Read *Jonathan Livingston Seagull* to fully understand the broader implications of the gull. But in the meantime, know that the gull portends a period of greater creative and personal freedom, as long as you do the work that's required. A trip for pleasure is indicated.

Hamster

You're best suited to a warm climate—Arizona, California, Florida. Being in a fast-paced, busy setting is upsetting to you and you would enjoy a slower, more rural setting much better. Hamster usually augurs well for pregnancy.

Hawk

You will have to call on your grace and agility very soon. You may be in a position where you have to defend yourself or your beliefs or an activity in which you're involved. You're seeking a higher truth and broader perspective.

Hedgehog

You're entering a period of solitude. You may feel like running and hiding somewhere, but don't do it. If you choose solitude, choose it because you want to and not because someone else forces you to do so. Health wise: Watch your weight. Protect yourself.

Hermit Crab

Growth. Change. Adaptability. You may be outgrowing your current circumstances. It's time to embrace change and experiment with new possibilities. Don't allow your own resistance to hold you back.

Heron

A career opportunity will present itself, allowing you to move to a warmer climate. If you already live in a warm climate, then stay where you are but consider a job change.

Horse

You need strength and endurance now in some area of your life. You're about to be courted and seduced—or perhaps you're the seducer—by someone for whom you feel an intensely sexual attraction. *See Wild Mustang under "Predictions."*

White Horse: You are surrounded by angels who are your protectors. Release your fears.

Red Horse: There will soon be an argument of a serious nature. On a worldly scale, you will hear of a terrible battle or war.

Hippopotamus

Group activities are important to you now. Network, make contacts. You don't hesitate to fight for what you believe. You may be interested in animals and ecology. Expect an increase in finances.

Hummingbird

You're entering a time of joy and prosperity and your dreams are reaching fruition. If you've been ill, Hummingbird augurs well for healing.

Hyena

Are you too opportunistic or not opportunistic enough? If you're invited in a group activity or to be a member of a team, be careful. These folks are hunters.

I

Ibex

If you're worried about an illness, your own or someone else's, be assured there will be a miraculous healing.

Ibis

You're adaptable to your surroundings and feel that you're the protector of your family. You need time to play and relax now. If you can get away for a few days, head for the water—a beach, a lake, a river—it doesn't matter as long as it's water. In ancient days, priests and seers got information from this bird, so there's an element of clairvoyance and intuitive awareness involved when Ibis enters your life. Spirituality is heightened.

Iguana

Don't use that tongue of yours to zap your enemies. Think before you speak. Your words may come back to haunt you. You're feeling more solitary now, so indulge yourself. You enjoy the warmth of the summer sun, but be sure your skin is protected.

Impala

You're extremely adaptive. If you're a man, then you have a "band of brothers" who are your support group. At this time, scent is important. It triggers childhood memories or memories that you associate with different periods of your life. Your sense of smell also heightens your libido! You may have to indulge that, too.

Insects

Look for the specific insect. In general, though, insects tend to be bothersome to most of us. So look for what bothers you most in your life and take action to correct it.

Itch Mite

Is someone getting under your skin? Unless you stand up for yourself this can go on forever. This mite causes scabies and spends its entire life on the host unless eliminated by medicinal ointment and sterilized clothing.

J

Jackal

Either you or someone around you is opportunistic. This isn't a bad thing unless it hurts others. Have a little faith in yourself and don't worry about what some think about you.

Jaguar

Like the lion and the bear, this animal is about personal power. You're on the right track when Jaguar appears. But move with stealth, in silence, and remain alert and aware. Think of this: The jaguar is the largest cat in the Western hemisphere, but also the least studied. It remains elusive.

Jay

Humor will see you through whatever is ailing you. When Jay appears, know that events are turning in your favor. Ignore gossip that you hear and don't gossip about others. For now, keep your own counsel.

Jellyfish

Spineless. Floating through life. Poisonous. Who's being passive-aggressive? Is that you? You need to reassess yourself and be less inclined to sting others.

K

Kangaroo

Don't hop around from one thing to another. Settle down to what you like best. You need balance in your life. If you have children, then they may need more guidance and protection at this time—or you may feel like being more protective now.

Key Deer

Your gentleness wins friends and supporters. Exercise caution when you drive and stay alert for danger. (Endangered)

Kinkajou

Independent, you find getting to the top is easy. You know there are many ways of getting there and are willing to investigate those methods.

Katy-Did

You have an appreciation for music. Dance and music are creative venues you should explore.

Koala

Are you being too aggressive with your peers? Take it easy or you may have to defend yourself tooth and toenail. You need to give someone close to you some room. You need to be single-minded and focused now, but also should expand your rather limited view of things.

Kingfisher

You're protected from negative energies, people, and situations that are around you. Kingfisher brings improved health, prosperity, and a special romance. Consider changing the colors of the rooms where you spend the most time.

The kingfisher is "Halcyon" from ancient Greek. Halcyon was also a faithful lover, according to Greek legend. She was the daughter of the God of the Winds and married Ceyx who was the son of the Day Star. He drowned at sea, but the Gods took pity on the lovers and changed them into Kingfishers. The expression "Halcyon Days" stems from reflecting days filled with pleasant and fond memories. So expect plenty of halcyon days!

L

Ladybug

Luck, harvest, good fortune, and transformation: It reads like a gypsy's fortune telling. But there's plenty to celebrate with this little bug around. Communal or family living is your safety catch.

Lemur

You're a sun-worshipper (who had better use sun block!) but have a distinct preference for the early morning hours. If you've been trying to get pregnant, Lemur says that April is the best month for achieving it. You would be happiest owning several acres somewhere. If you're a woman in a committed relationship, you're the dominant partner. Timing: look to 136 days.

Leopard

You are very powerful, but must learn to use that power. You tire easily, so test yourself before going for the long haul.

Lice

Are you suffering thoughts of anger, worrying about poor finances or being poverty stricken? This stress can cause you illness. Get to the root of the worry and watch all the stress vanish.

Lion

Your family is most important. You find great interest in community affairs and like being in the forefront of things. Any career having to do with family or government affairs could be possible. If you're a man, are you doing your fair share in a partnership? Lions are also about personal power. Are you hiding your power? Abusing it? Misusing it? Or is someone using his or her power against you? If you dream of a lion, take note of what the lion is doing in the dream and your relationship to the lion. That will provide insight on your relationship to your own power.

Asiatic lions, a sub-species of lions that split from their African counterparts some one hundred thousand years ago, now number about 300 and live on a 560-square mile sanctuary in India's Gir Forest. More than 2,000 people live within the lion sanctuary and recent attacks on residents and their livestock have created an atmosphere of terror that inadvertently endangers the lions. These lions don't reproduce prolifically and have a small gene pool, which means that 70-80 percent of sperm is deformed, which sometimes leads to infertility.

Lizard

You blend in well with your surroundings and for now, that's to your advantage. Watch. Observe. Be still when you must be. Slow down the pace of your life.

Llama

Stamina. Sturdiness. Adorable but bad-tempered. If you feel you're overworked and overburdened, then do something about it. Start delegating responsibility to others. Ask for help when you need it.

Lorikeet

You're quite the social creature right now and that's exactly what you need. Get out into the world. Wear bright, bold colors. But watch your fondness for sweets! (Scarlet breasted lorikeet is endangered.)

Lovebird

You're smart and sassy and you know it. A special someone is headed into your life who shares your love of music.

Macaw

You're in for a dramatic, demanding time. Your communication skills are going to be more important than ever. But don't just talk—be a good listener, too. In captivity, macaws need faithful, loving care and attention. Without it, domesticated Macaws suffer greatly—and so do we. (Hyacinth macaw is endangered.)

Magpie

You're curious, skillful, can talk to anyone about anything, and use whatever is at hand to get ahead. It may be time to study metaphysical and occult knowledge.

Manatee

Your gentleness is practically legendary among your friends and family and right now, those qualities will get you farther than you imagine. But it's time to slow down the pace of your life, get your priorities straight, and remind yourself that life is meant to be joyful. (Endangered)

Martin

Your spiritual beliefs are important to you now. They provide a foundation that you need. Expect good luck at home and concerning your children.

Mink

You have a tendency to be unsociable and hostile to those around you. Lighten up! Quit being angry at the world. Have a little fun!

Mockingbird

You're very territorial and don't like anyone invading your space. For the time being, stay where you are, doing whatever you're doing. It's not time yet for change.

Mole

You should be in tune with spiritual healing or laying-on-of-hands. You sense afflictions by touch and it would benefit you to know herb lore and reflexology. Develop your abilities to expose and unearth anxieties and fears—your own and others'. Your intuition and predictive abilities are especially strong now.

Mongoose

Do not be concerned about your enemies. You will defeat those snakes in the grass. Forge ahead.

Monkey

You're changeable and often "hang by your thumbs" while working on a project. You can control the situation, though, because you usually have other options in reserve. Don't allow anyone to make a fool of you.

Moose

You may be slow, but you have a built-in radar to detect things. No one can pull the wool over your eyes. In some situation or relationship, you're being too aggressive or unpredictable. It's time to back off. Something isn't being taken as seriously as it should be.

Mourning Dove

The mourning dove is a sign of love, peace, and contentment in your life. You value mutual love, loyalty, and respect. Love issues will be resolved within the next few weeks. Be patient.

Mosquito

What's really bugging you? It's probably the small, nitpicky things—a whole string of them. Tackle them one at a time, then figure out the root belief or emotion that has brought the events about, and change it.

Moth

The sight of a moth is a reminder of the Biblical injunction not to accumulate material goods that moths and rust can consume and thieves can steal. It's wiser to lay up spiritual treasure in your heart. The fact that a moth's wings are laid back suggests that you should not be so "laid-back" that you fall asleep on the job of inner work.

Clothing Moth: Something's eating away at you. Let it go before it consumes you or leaves you so emotionally damaged you will find it nearly impossible to recover.

Mouse

Pay attention to details, but don't be so fastidious that you neglect the big things. Try not to accumulate junk and stuff that you don't need. If your attic or closets are filled with things you haven't used in months, then have a garage sale.

Mynah

You are skilled as a mimic and enjoy being "on stage." You're looking for a life mate, not a fling, and would like to have kids and a family. You have fun as a practical jokester but remember not to carry this play too far.

N

Newt

You're basically a "cold fish" and don't respond well to your mate. Perhaps you should try finding out about his/her dislikes.

Nightingale

You are such a tattletale. Be reminded that gossip has its paybacks. Although you have that "singing" voice, hide for your own protection.

O

Octopus

You're a master of camouflage and while that ability may get you far, don't let it get to the point where you no longer know who you are. Your parenting skills need some work now. It could be that your libido has distracted you from parenting responsibilities. For health, Octopus is an excellent omen: It means regeneration. It doesn't get much better than that!

Opossum

C'mon, stop hiding your abilities. Show what you know and be proud that you know it!

Orangutan

You are remarkably intelligent and adaptable to any scene. Although a part of you would like to get married and settle down, another part of you enjoys your solitude. Which will it be—wedded bliss or solitude?

Oryx

Conserve your energy, and if you can't stand the heat, get out of the kitchen. Wait for a more suitable time to take care of your affairs.

Osprey

You sometimes set yourself apart from others and take the moral high road. You're adept at seeing the larger picture, can spot an opportunity a mile away, and tend to be something of an opportunist at times. You're most successful when adapting yourself to a situation. You can overcome anyone who wishes you ill will.

Ostrich

Are you pretending that an unpleasant situation doesn't exist? Rather than trying to avoid whatever it is, confront it, solve it, and move on.

Otter

You are extremely energetic and work very hard to maintain your lifestyle. Good food and plenty of it is important to maintain that energy. Choose a home on or near the water for peace and contentment. If you are female, you need and love to romp with your children.

Owl

Continue your education. You'll gain wisdom and skills that you need. You may hear of a death or tragedy, but don't be fearful of something you don't understand. News is on the way.

Ox

You're a hard, tenacious worker and, to some extent, have insulated yourself from the pain that the world inflicts. Your children, however, don't have the ability yet to do what you do; teach by example.

Oyster

You're somewhat sedentary and need to get to work. Set goals. Discover your passions. Open your heart.

Oyster Catcher

Being noisy and gregarious, you do well in a social atmosphere. You hammer away to reach your goal. You are family oriented and protective of those you love.

P

Panda

Okay, you're cute and everyone knows that. But you need to be more than cute to achieve anything. The irony is that you're not superficial and can get to the heart of a problem. In terms of health: Is your wrist bothering you? Is carpal tunnel syndrome a possibility? Get it checked out. Try alternative therapies rather than surgery. You may want to try a vegetarian diet for awhile. (Endangered)

Panther

You're solitary and enjoy traveling. When you socialize, it's mostly with family. You're tough to get to know. An opportunity to move to a warmer climate will have to be considered soon. (Endangered)

Parrot

A stranger will try to deceive you by flattery. You like the flattery, but don't get sucked in. Communication counts now.

Peacock

Clever and shy, you're fascinated by things or people who are harmful to you. Your arrogance and strutting sometimes cause people to dislike you until they discover it's just a mask for your shyness. Show your more beautiful side more often, but do not allow yourself to think that your beauty will take you anywhere you want to go.

Pelican

When taking care of business you seldom miss the mark. You don't need to talk a lot in attempting to get the job done. With you, "actions speak louder than words." Keep up the good work. You are doing A-Okay.

Penguin

You're very social right now. When this bird appears, it suggests you are someone who is gregarious and probably a little vain. Maybe you should pay more attention to those who are important to you. If you're a man, it's time for you to take a major role in the care of your kids. Whether you're male or female, you should consider, well, how you look. Would it kill you to dress up a little?!

Pheasant

This one can go either way: it's time to strut your stuff or it's time to hide. Only you know for sure which one.

Phoenix

You'll overcome impossible odds. In the romance area: You're about to meet someone with whom you share a deep past-life connection. No telling how this relationship will unfold. A lot of it depends on the karma you share.

Pig

Abundance. Prosperity. You're in for a nice financial run. You had better come up against a sticky situation with intelligence and leadership skills. If you've been wallowing in self-pity lately, get over it.

Pigeon

If things are hectic in your life there will soon be peace. You are creative, a novel thinker, and observant. So use these qualities to achieve what you desire.

Porcupine

You're feeling a bit defensive lately. Your family and friends know to stay out of your way. However, you're really good at protecting yourself and others respect you for that, even if they're intimidated. Chill. You might want to smooth down those quills. Don't take things so personally.

Prairie Dog

You enjoy living in a community and excel in community activities, even as a volunteer. Continue to help those in need. You will be rewarded in due time. You can create wonders when you work with others like yourself. But you'll probably have to do it in secret and keep it underground. Constantly watch out for intruders who may not love what you are doing.

Pronghorn

Be ever vigilant and communicate danger to others. You have excellent insight into future trends. You will be using those attributes to assist others in their lives in the near future. Don't be afraid to say what you are psychically seeing and feeling.

Q

Quail

Be mindful of danger. You can safely escape when threatened. Don't hesitate in times of crisis. Make a lot of noise to frighten off the invader, either natural or manmade.

R

Rabbit

You are sensitive and artistic. You are a family loving person and are likely to have many children. You have the power to see things in another realm. You will have the opportunity to teach soon. Use your own special "magic" with your young students. They will laugh and enjoy the lesson. An excellent omen for pregnancy.

Eastern Cottontail: This is a sign of rebirth or birth. Your vegetarian diet is good for you. You're very adaptable to your environment and can fit in anywhere.

Raccoon

You are adaptable, curious, determined, and intelligent. You have great manual dexterity and would excel at a task that involves using your hands. You love the water and cool mountain streams, and this would be a good vacation location. You're versatile and could be a "Patch Adams" with medicine and magic. Take advantage of the opportunities that will soon be upon you.

Ram

You can invoke illumination and healing to the person who is coming to you for strength and assistance. You will need to be strong if that person is depressed. Your lady love will be speaking to you soon about having a child. The term "horny little devil" really applies to you. You need to make the woman in your life happy. The ram is the animal associated with the zodiac sign Aries. There's an element of the trailblazer in you.

Rat

You are very strong and can travel all over the world with ease. You have lasting power and will be successful. Don't be afraid to step into new places. The significance of a rat depends a lot on what kind and where it is. A lab rat signifies suffering, and knowledge gained at someone else's expense. A sewer rat indicates feisty survival skills. A rat in an inappropriate locale—like your kitchen!—may be a warning about blocking up the holes in your life where danger can enter. Most rats represent corruption at some level, but a pet rat, if it is loved and treated kindly, is a sign of hope and of wholesome interaction with the natural world.

Raven

"Nevermore," said the raven in Poe's poem. And that should be your mantra. Be wary of people who seek to involve you in things that don't please the masses (consensus reality). You'll have ample opportunities to help others with your predictions, but you may have to give up something that is dear to you.

Redheaded Woodpecker

You forage for your family. That's fine, as long as you accept the role. You may be heading south for the winter, joining the ranks of snowbirds. You're persistent, communicative, and although it's sometimes good to peck away at things, it may become annoying to others. When it does, back off.

Reindeer

You bring hope and joy to others in their darkest hours. You are compassionate and kind. You may volunteer or work for a hospice organization. Don't pass up this opportunity to help others and to bring a measure of happiness to their final days.

Resplendent Quetzal

You're a survivor. That just about says it all, doesn't it?

Rhinoceros

You're an old soul and that means you have the wisdom you need to move forward. Even if your pace isn't especially swift, your energy is positive and can infuse others with a sense of personal power and strength. However, take care that your shortsightedness doesn't hold you back.

Roadrunner

You have great prowess in facing your enemies. You are persistent until victory is in sight and wear them down with your staying power. Have "heart," for victory is imminent. Whatever problems you are facing will disappear.

Robin

You love and need music and may have singing talent. Some new happenings will give your life a boost, with spring as the time to watch for. The worst is over. Enjoy the sunshine, but don't take it *too* easy. Still gotta get those worms!

S

Salamander

Do your emotions need grounding? You may be going through a "trial by fire," but as long as you stick to your principles, you will come out okay. If you've been experiencing skin rashes and blemishes, a visit to the dermatologist is in order. (Endangered)

Salmon

When you dream of Salmon, wisdom and inspiration are gained. You may be returning to your roots or doing genealogical research.

Scarab Beetle

You're entering a period in your life when the mundane becomes sacred. You don't need to carry anyone else's responsibilities. Be assured that you can proceed with power and determination on your spiritual path.

Scorpion

Secretive, psychic, and penetrating. Scorpion rules the sign of Scorpio, the most secretive sign in the zodiac. You have intense feelings about a relationship or situation and must draw on your innate wisdom to resolve an issue. Be careful that your words don't sting others.

Seahorse

If contemplating a family, don't be concerned about parenthood. As a father you will tend your offspring with loving kindness and understanding. If you are female, you will have healing abilities for your children, especially those who might suffer from breathing or asthmatic problems.

Seal

You're built for speed and will accomplish what has to be done in a hurry. If you're a woman, try to take more time with your children and focus your energies.

Sea Turtle

You may be taking a long trip related to an investigation or research. Time is definitely on your side. But you, like everyone else, may be in danger of losing your freedom to move around as you please. (Endangered)

Shark

Perpetual motion. Impersonal cruelty. Doing what comes naturally. Tough-skinned. You'll come through situations as the winner.

Sheep

Be a leader and don't suffer the consequences of indecisiveness. This can be a new beginning for you if you assert yourself. You're sure-footed.

Shrew

This is one of nature's few venomous mammals. That shrew at home or work may be ready to bite down on you. Constant nagging from someone close to you leaves you feeling depleted and depressed. Don't allow this to happen. Protect yourself.

Shrike

You are fast to "go in for the kill" to get what you want. You need to become more spiritual if you wish to have a happy life.

Shrimp

Your sense of touch is important when selecting your clothing. Color, too, is special for you. You gravitate toward golds and yellows. When Shrimp pops into your life, months that end in R are important.

Skunk

You need to be more self-assured and assertive. Show respect and demand respect. Scent is important to you and can trigger memories of past lives or of early childhood. Scent may also be important in a new romance or sexual encounter. Cooperation will take you farther than outright aggression. However, if you're cornered, have courage to act on your own instincts.

Skylark

Is it time for you and your family to move out of the city and into the country? A rural setting will suit your needs. A happy time is ahead.

Sloth

Your metabolism is slow these days and you're feeling lethargic. Get out and exercise. Take vitamin supplements. If you're overweight, it's time to go on a diet.

Slug

Are you taking the path most difficult for you? Do you avoid conflict or confrontation unless it benefits you? It is time to look beyond yourself and to the needs and feelings of others.

Snail

You may be conflicted about your sexuality. Don't hide who you are. You won't be truly happy until you make that decision and follow your heart.

Snake

Your spiritual activities are heightened; your dreams become more lucid. Snake also represents healing, strength, nocturnal activities, sexuality, transformation, and is the spirit of life and death.

Sparrow

When Sparrow appears in your life, you're entering a period of greater adaptability, new opportunities, and new creativity, possibly through music. The next eleven to fourteen days are important in terms of your creative endeavors.

Spider

You're entering an intensely creative period of your life. Part of your success will be due to your ability to camouflage yourself, to blend in with a crowd, and yet to stand out from the crowd in terms of what you produce.

Black Widow Spider: You may be shy, but if you're provoked by someone, you know how to defend yourself.

Squirrel

You are quite sociable. You can learn much by observing those around you. You are a good communicator and will have an opportunity in the next three months to work in a field such as newspaper, radio, or TV reporting.

Stag

You can lead the one who follows you to a place of wonder and magic, either spiritually or physically.

Starfish

You often act without thinking. Back up, look at the situation, and then you will make a wiser decision on how to act.

Stork

Do you feel that you're in emotional turmoil? Return to your roots and remember the innocence within you. You're giving birth to new attitudes and activities in your life. For higher energy, start taking those dance lessons, even if you feel you already know how to dance. Yoga would be beneficial for you, too, particularly balance postures called The Crane or The Stork, as well as a series of postures known as the Sun Salutation.

Swallow

Be careful of people who say one thing and mean another. Be aware of what people are saying and not how they are saying it. Dismiss those who provoke you. You're not required to allow anyone to hurt or anger you. By the same token, don't stir another to wrath.

Swan

Keep your distance from someone you're attracted to until that person shows his or her true colors. Sometimes, beauty really is skin deep. However, once you're sure about who this person really is, the romance may quickly turn into a lifelong relationship and commitment.

T

Tarantula

Trust your own feelings. You are very sensitive to the undercurrent around you. When you feel threatened, find a way to distract the source of that threat so that you can escape. Throw off old ways and try the new.

Tasmanian Devil

Your reputation for being ruthless and vicious is unfounded. Don't be concerned about other people's clutter. Tend to your own business and let other people tend to theirs.

Termite

Get down to earth, shed those wings and "dig in." Perform the duties assigned you and you will make things in your life grow. A second divination suggests that if these insects invade your home, rough times may be ahead.

Thunderbird

This represents power, great strength, and leadership. You're here to fulfill your destiny.

Tick

What's attacking your joy and pep in life? It's possible that you're not paying attention to your health. Early recognition of health problems can bring about remedies and cures. You need to examine friendships and loves. Tick symbolizes the common sense need to be careful, even about small things. But it also symbolizes the danger of inflating fears way out of proportion to the risk. Like a tick, fear can be a parasite, sucking the life out of you. The message here is: Do want you want to do, take sensible precautions, and don't let your fears cripple your enjoyment of life.

Tiger

Personal power is the issue. Are you letting someone else take yours away? If so, take steps now to remedy the situation. Stand up for yourself.

Tit-Mouse

You are good at collecting from others to build your own nest. You pick their brains and make good use any information that they wish to share.

Toucan

The toucan has a huge beak but isn't overbalanced due to the holes in it. Are you feeling overbalanced in work or other phases of your life? When this colorful bird appears, it's a sign that everything in your life is A-Okay.

Turkey

Share your bounty and harvest with others. Trust in the abundance of the universe and know that whatever you give to others returns to you threefold.

Turtle

You will have a long life with many wonderful relationships. You will be awakened to a number of opportunities coming to you soon through your senses. Look and listen to what your instincts are telling you.

Every year, more than 10,000 endangered green turtles make their way to the Great Barrier Reef of Australia to lay eggs. They come from as far away as Papua New Guinea and Indonesia and have thus earned the name, "ancient mariners."

There is a great deal of mythology which exists in regard to the turtle. In the Far East, the shell was a symbol of heaven, and the square underside was a symbol of earth. The turtle's magic united heaven and earth. In the West, early Christians did not like turtles, and they viewed them as symbolizing evil forces during war. In Greece turtles were once believed to be citizens of hell. One old Indian woman believed the world was being supported by a giant turtle. The turtle symbolizes longevity and immortality. For women, the turtle is a powerful symbol for fertility, long life, and perseverance. It is even considered able to defy death.

Snapping Turtle: Is it you, or somebody else? One of you is irritable and needs to be handled carefully. If it's you, try kind words instead of biting the other person's head off. If it's someone else, don't stick your nose into their business!

U

Unicorn

Even though the unicorn is a mythological creature, people do dream of them. If you dream of a unicorn, it's likely that magical situations and relationships are on their way into your life. When Unicorn appears, head over to your local library and buy Peter Beagle's book, *The Last Unicorn*.

One favorite legend about the unicorn goes something like this:

One day, when a little girl (Elaine) was out playing in the woods, she stumbled upon a young unicorn. They became wonderful friends. She even named her unicorn friend "Moraine," after her mother. She played with her friend until she was sixteen years old, then didn't see the unicorn for four years.

During that time someone got into the village and ate all of the sheep. The hunters believed the unicorns were guilty and were sent out to kill them. Moraine ran away, deep into the woods, and lived there in the hope that one day her friend, Elaine, would come and play with her again.

One day, Moraine was out for a walk and saw Elaine with a handsome young man. Moraine was excited and ran to play with her. Moraine didn't know what to do when Elaine refused. But Elaine explained that she was now married and no longer had time for childish games. Moraine was so heartbroken that she went away and hid, never to be seen again.

We continue to reject animals emotionally. Because we don't accord them rights, they are dying off and becoming extinct. The unicorn is the perfect example.

Vicuna (South American Camel)

You need to live near an arid area. Retirement will soon be at hand, so start considering Florida, the Southwest, or a comparable location.

Vulture

Strongly tied to life and death. In terms of work and profession, you could do very well as a funeral director or in the health field. When Vulture appears, there are lessons to be learned and prizes to be won, even from loss and hardship. Get your digestive system checked.

Wasp

Self-sufficiency. Make the best of what you have. If the wasp stings you, however, look at the areas of your life where you feel you have been injured and seek to heal the wounds.

Water Dragon

You're a good swimmer and can out swim the competition when troubles arise. You appear to be formidable but will avoid a fight if possible.

Weasel (Ferret)

You're energetic and filled with mischief. Be careful of those practical jokes because they can get you in a lot of trouble. You bring much joy to those about you and need to continue being funny. You are a loner and may soon be asked to do some solitary snooping in your office. Go for it! You make a good spy.

Whale

Some problems are too big to handle alone. Get some help. Don't allow pride to keep you from sharing your worries with another. They will deem it an honor that you asked them to help and will enlighten you. (Endangered)

Whip-poor-will

Legend has it that this bird sucks milk from goats. This is due to the shape of the mouth. This night singer seems to be a sign that you should be doing something musical—singing, playing an instrument, or selling musical instruments. You appreciate nightclubs and karaoke. Your creative adrenaline may be much stronger at night.

Whooping Crane

Are you paying enough attention to your family? If not, then get on the case. Kids grow up faster than you think! You would benefit at this time from yoga and a regular exercise routine. (Endangered)

Wolf

To be successful, you must learn proper conduct. You need to learn your place in the society hierarchy. Heed these lessons and benefit from them. You have much to teach yourself and others. (Endangered)

Wolverine

You are fearless and often too domineering. Be kinder in your methods with others if you don't want to lose friends and family. (Endangered)

Woodpecker (redheaded)

Woodpecker's appearance is telling you to lay in for the winter, with supplies and appropriate clothing, or turn into a "snow bird" and head south for the winter. The importance of communication is heightened now. (Endangered)

Wrens

Your nature is bold and aggressive, but you love being near others. You are a good parent and very protective of those you love.

Z

Zebra

Quit trancing out and look about you. You have keen hearing and excellent perceptions and need to use both to know what is happening around you. Use your seniority to move ahead. Sometimes you've just got to be who you've got to be, regardless of what other people think of you. But try to remember that they've got to be who they are, too. (Endangered)

Animals of The Bible

Ass: John: 12: 14.

Bees and Lion: Judges 14: 7-9.

Camel, Hare, Coney, and Swine: Deut.: 14: 7-8.

Cattle: These animals were first mentioned in Genesis and appear several times throughout the Bible.

Cock: Luke: 23: 61.

Dog: Exodus: 11

Dove: Dove, too, was sent out a number of times to search for dry land and finally returned with an olive branch in its mouth, signaling that the flood waters were receding. Genesis: 8: 8-12.

Eagle, Osprey, Owl, Hawk, Kite: Deut.: 14: 12-17.

Hart, Roebuck, Wild Goat, Wild Ox, and Chamois: Deut: 14: 5.

Lamb: In Christianity, the lamb represents Christ as both suffering and triumphant; It is a sacrificial animal and symbolizes innocence, gentleness, and purity. When lying down with the lion, it can mean a state of paradise. It also symbolizes meekness, sweetness, and forgiveness. The Lamb of God is also mentioned throughout the Bible.

Locust: Exodus: 10: 4, 12-14.

Raven: Raven was first to leave Noah's Ark after the flood to search for dry land. Genesis 8: 7.

Serpent: This snake in the grass is the fallen angel known as Satan who entered the garden of Eden and convinced Eve to eat the forbidden fruit. Genesis 3: 1, 14.

Appendix

~~~~~~

T his appendix is a basic resource for books—nonfiction and fiction—movies, communities, websites, and people that deal with topics covered in *Animal Totems*.

Books

A Cat Named Darwin, by William Jordan

And the Animals Will Teach You: Discovering Ourselves Through Our Relationships with Animals, by Margot Lasher

Animal Grace: Entering a Spiritual Relationship with Our Fellow Creatures, by Mary Lou Randour

Animals As Teachers and Healers, by Susan Chernak McElroy

Animal Liberation, by Peter Singer

Animal Miracles, by Brad Steiger and Sherry Hansen Steiger

Animal Speak, by Ted Andrews

Animal Talk, by Penelope Smith

The Call of the Wild, by Jack London

Charlotte's Web, by E.B. White

Childrens' Past Lives, by Carol Bowman

Crossing Over, by John Edwards

Dogs That Know When Their Owners Are Coming Home, by
Rupert Sheldrake

Dolphins, Telepathy and Underwater Birthing, by Timothy Wyllie

The Dolphin Within, by Olivia de Bergerac

Dominion: The Power of Man, the Suffering of Animals, and the Call to Mercy,
by Matthew Scully

The Hidden Life of Dogs, by Elizabeth Marshall Thomas

The I Ching or Chinese Book of Changes, by Richard Wilhelm

Intimate Nature: the Bond Between Women and Animals, edited by Linda
Hogan, Deena Metzger, and Brenda Peterson

Journey of the Pink Dolphins, by Sy Montgomery

Kindred Spirits, by Allen M. Schoen

Love, Miracles and Animal Healing, by Allen M. Schoen and Pam Proctor

Memories, Dreams and Reflections, by Carl Jung

The Moon by Whale Light, by Diane Ackerman

The Naked Ape, by Desmond Morris

The Nature of Personal Reality, by Jane Roberts

The Octopus and the Orangutan, by Eugene Linden

Old Yeller, by Fred Gibson

The Parrot Who Owns Me, by Joanna Burger

The Pig Who Sang to the Moon, by Jeffrey Moussaieff Masson

Pilgrim at Tinker's Creek, by Annie Dillard

Power Tarot, by Trish MacGregor and Phyllis Vega

The Presence of the Past, by Rupert Sheldrake

Priceless: The Vanishing Beauty of a Fragile Planet, by Bradley Trevor Greive

Return from Heaven, by Carol Bowman

Seth Speaks, by Jane Roberts

Seven Experiments that Could Change the World, by Rupert Sheldrake

Synchronicity, by Carl Jung

The Ten Trusts, by Jane Goodall

Watchers, by Dean Koontz

When Elephants Weep: The Emotional Lives of Animals, by Jeffrey Moussaieff Masson and Susan McCarthy

Movies

Andre

Babe

Beethoven

The Black Stallion

Charlotte's Web

Day of the Dolphin

Dead Again

Dragonfly

Dragonheart

Fluke

Fly Away Home

Free Willy (all three of them)

Homeward Bound

The Horse Whisperer

Jacob's Ladder

Lady and the Tramp

Old Yeller

101 Dalmatians

Shiloh

Sliding Doors

Spirit

21 Grams

Zeus and Roxanne

Psychics/Mediums

Millie Gemondo: 304-584-4233. Call for an appointment.

Hazel Burley: 386-228-3826. Call for an appointment.

Animal-Related Websites

www.alleycat.org: Alley Cats

www.aspca.com: Society for the Prevention of Cruelty to Animals

www.bancruelfarms.org: Ban Cruel Farms

www.bestfriends.org: the nation's largest sanctuary for abused and
abandoned animals

www.care2.com: the "yahoo" for people who care about the environment

www.defenders.org: Defenders of Wildlife website

www.drschoen.com: website for author and veterinarian Allen Schoen

www.islanddolphincare.org: swimming with dolphins in Key Largo, Florida

www.mathewscully.com: website for author of *Dominion*

www.mercyforanimals.org: Mercy for Animals

www.peta.org: People for the Ethical Treatment of Animals

www.sentientbeings.org: Sentient beings

www.sheldrake.org: website for biologist and author Rupert Sheldrake

www.VegForLife.org: vegetarian alternatives

Index

STONE AGE WISDOM
By Tom Crockett
ISBN 1-59233-014-2
$15.95 (£9.99)
Paperback; 272 pages
Available wherever books are sold

"In this remarkable book, Tom Crockett takes his reader through a shamanic journey, but he does not teach the traditional shaman's forms of practice. Instead, he describes the evolution of 'urban shamanism,' and how ancient wisdom traditions can be used in contemporary practices. Especially useful are the exercises, ceremonies, and rituals that Crockett prescribes for his readers; especially fascinating are his chapters on dreams and visions. But readers need to heed this warning: Your belief systems may never be the same again!"
—Stanley Krippner, Ph.D., co-author of the *Extraordinary Dreams and How to Work with Them* and co-editor of *Varieties of Anomalous Experience*

PUT YOUR LIFE IN BALANCE WITH THE WISDOM OF THE SHAMAN

What does it mean to live in balance? Most people know what it feels like to live out of balance. The fast pace of modern life has left many of us without roots or a sense of connectedness to life around us. Shamanism can bring spiritual fulfillment back into the urban contemporary life. In *Stone Age Wisdom*, you'll learn how to incorporate the basic principles of shamanism into your everyday life, bringing meaning to your most basic tasks.

You'll learn to:
- **DREAM**—to be open to and understand the wisdom of the dreaming
- **VISION-SHIFT**—to develop the ability to sense that everything is alive
- **JOURNEY**—to enter into dialogue with spirit
- **SHAPE-SHIFT**—to practice the art of change
- **CONDUCT RITUALS**—to mediate between the seen and the unseen worlds
- **DREAM-WEAVE**—to direct will and intention through embodied prayer and creative action

ABOUT THE AUTHOR
Tom Crockett has been engaged in shamanic spiritual practice for more than ten years. He conducts workshops and edits a newsletter for urban shamanic practitioners. He is the author of *The Artist Inside: A Spiritual Guide to Cultivating Your Creative Self.* He lives in Virginia.